An Introduction to
KNOWLEDGE
INFORMATION
STRATEGY

From Business Intelligence to
Knowledge Sciences

An Introduction to
KNOWLEDGE INFORMATION STRATEGY

From Business Intelligence to Knowledge Sciences

Editors

Akira Ishikawa
Aoyama Gakuin University, Japan

Juro Nakagawa
Nihon University, Japan

NEW JERSEY · LONDON · SINGAPORE · BEIJING · SHANGHAI · HONG KONG · TAIPEI · CHENNAI

Published by

World Scientific Publishing Co. Pte. Ltd.
5 Toh Tuck Link, Singapore 596224
USA office: 27 Warren Street, Suite 401-402, Hackensack, NJ 07601
UK office: 57 Shelton Street, Covent Garden, London WC2H 9HE

British Library Cataloguing-in-Publication Data
A catalogue record for this book is available from the British Library.

Translation by Takako Iwaki/TranNet KK, Japan

ISBN 978-981-4324-42-7

In-house Editor: Yvonne Tan

Typeset by Stallion Press
Email: enquiries@stallionpress.com

Printed in Singapore by World Scientific Printers.

Preface

The recent world financial crisis derived from the subprime incidents, followed by the sharp economic downturn, can be attributed to the lack of understanding and decisive shortage of learning power regarding BI (Business Intelligence).

Believing in the consistent increases of residential prices, as well as the consistent increases of stock prices, is not very realistic, and is one of the notable examples of prediction failure which is the very basis of intelligence. Many people have studied the realm of forecasting, particularly in economics and business administration, and a great number of professionals are working in this area. Despite this reality, why have such unbelievable subprime incidents taken place and why have so many investors and consumers been victimized?

It appears that business leaders, professionals, and specialists have not strived to learn the lessons of the past, notably from the financial crisis of the 1920s and the more recent bubble collapses. By using what is called CDS (Credit Default Swap), which is a highly risky means, many financial institutions in the US and Europe have been involved in these subprime incidents. In order to recover to the previous state, intelligence creation, evaluation, and management need to be studied seriously.

From the 1980s to the 1990s, SIS (Strategic Information Systems) had been very popular. Now, with the evolution of IT, including information and communication networks, the PC, and many other mobile devices as well as the explosive increases in information content, the scope and depth of information analysis has increased dramatically in parallel with the importance of BI. It is very ironic that such a valuable resource was not referenced in advance to minimize the financial crisis.

In today's advanced information society where financial capitalism is deeply imbedded, as competition becomes more intense, the country, society, organization, and individuals that control information can gain a decisive advantage by benefiting from the differences in the quality of information. The core of this information is knowledge information, that is to say, intelligence. How to create, foster, share, and manage knowledge that is the basis of such business intelligence is a matter to be resolved by administrators, managers, executives, and employees in the governments, industries, universities, and NGOs in the 21st century. In particular, for those who are engaged in organizational creation and information analysis, continuous and evolving learning and discovery are indispensable.

This book encompasses three knowledge domains — BI, Knowledge, and Crisis and Risk Management — which are most important for business survival nowadays. The authors explore how to create and manage intelligence from different viewpoints, with an emphasis on enhancing competitive intelligence from information creation as well as capturing the platform of knowledge sciences that are the basis of knowledge management.

Accordingly, Part I begins with an introduction to BI and the theoretical and practical backgrounds of BI beyond the scope of traditional competitive intelligence, while Part II further explores theoretical and practical BI on the basis of knowledge management and knowledge sciences, connected with crisis and risk management. Part III is devoted to the application of BI to military and non-military areas, ranging from industries such as manufacturing, distribution, finance, insurance, communications, and healthcare, to Japan's Horse Racing Association.

The authors of Part I consist of Professor Juro Nakagawa who established the Business Intelligence Society of Japan and is devoted to the promotion and diffusion of BI, and Mr. Kunio Hashida (Chapter 6, Section 3) who is a representative in Japan of the

Information Industry Association of France and is therefore well-versed in French BI.

Part II is written by Professor Emeritus Akira Ishikawa, Aoyama Gakuin University and Honorary President of the Crisis and Risk Management Society of Japan, who is popular with his publications on Strategic Information Systems and the relevant Nikkei Video on Technology of Strategic Management.

As for Part III, Chapter 11 is written by Professor Tetsuo Narita, former executive of Japan IBM Application Solution and Visiting Professor of Kanazawa Institute of Technology, who for the first time introduces the Way of Thinking and Cases of Applications of IBM Business Intelligence; whereas Chapter 12 is written by Yoshio Suginoo, former professor of Japan Defense Academy, whose book entitled *The Essentials of Failure* has been a bestseller. It is said that Former Prime Minister Yasuhiro Nakasone thought very highly of this book.

The authors hope that this book will help strengthen the collection, sharing, management, and evaluation of BI so that the revitalization and evolution of Japan and the present world can be successfully accomplished.

November 2008
Co-editor and Author, Akira Ishikawa

Contents

PART I

PART 1

Chapter 1

What is Business Intelligence?

1. Value-Adding, Competitive Intelligence

In recent years, the source of power has shifted from land, finance and capital to intellectual capital; in the 21st century, society will be governed by intelligence, knowledge and wisdom. In the future, the power of a nation will be based not only on its territory, population, military strength, products and finance, but also on intelligence, technology, knowledge, education, intellectual prowess, software and culture, which will form the major factors of progress and development of the nation and society. Faced with this transition, Japan needs to establish new strategies to renovate and rebuild the nation.

In this respect, study of business intelligence and competitive intelligence is highly necessary. Business Intelligence (BI) refers to information that is collected, organized, evaluated and analyzed; thus value-added, it can contribute to decision-making. Competitive Intelligence (CI) is part of BI; CI enhances the value of BI further, giving it a competitive edge.

To have BI, it is necessary to clearly define the purpose at hand when collecting information; to secure reliable information sources; to assess, examine, and analyze the obtained information; to draw up and make use of effective reports; and to audit the intelligence. This process of refining information into intelligence is called the "intelligence cycle".

Dr. Benjamin Gilad, former Associate Professor at Rutgers University, divides the processes of BI into five parts — collection, evaluation, storing, analysis, and dissemination — in his book, *The Business*

Intelligence System. That is to say, the information collected from the government and industry should be evaluated, stored, analyzed, and disseminated.

On the other hand, Mr. Mark Lowenthal, a former CIA analyst and a current lecturer of intelligence at Columbia University, introduces five phases of the intelligence cycle — planning/direction, collection, processing/exploitation, analysis/production, and dissemination — in his book, *Intelligence from Secrets to Policy* (see Figure 1).

Dr. Stevan Dedijer of Lund University, Sweden, divides BI into four processes — retrieval and collection, storing, analysis, and presentation — while Mr. Herbert E. Meyer, ex-Vice Chairman of the

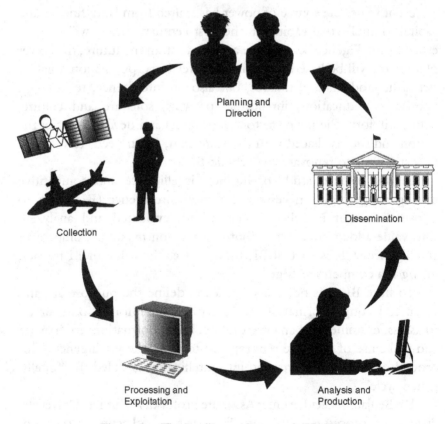

Figure 1: The Intelligence Process: A CIA View

Source: Central Intelligence Agency, *A Consumer's Handbook to Intelligence*, September 1993.

National Intelligence Council, defines BI as information to be collected, selected, analyzed, organized and disseminated to fulfill unique needs of a particular company's policy-making (Herbert E. Meyer, *Real-World Intelligence*).

2. The Methodology of Business Intelligence

For BI strategy, it is vital to have information analysis ability to make the best use of information for corporate strategy, recognizing crises and opportunities lying ahead, and preparing the company for them. In the US and Europe, corporations make use of techniques developed by the CIA and the intelligence community as management methods to refine information into intelligence.

Herbert E. Meyer divides the process into the following four stages:

(1) Distinguish relevant information from irrelevant information.
(2) Select necessary information and store it.
(3) Process the collected information.
(4) Report the results, conclusion, assessment, and prediction, so that it can contribute to top management's decision-making.

Through the above four phases, i.e., selection, gathering, processing and dissemination, information becomes value-added intelligence that generates profits.

Companies collect and analyze information for the following purposes:

(1) To collect information about competitors, industries, governments and nations for management strategy;
(2) To collect and analyze background information, such as information about technology, politics, economy, society and culture;
(3) To observe the changing business environment and keep track of trends; and
(4) To monitor the trends of suppliers of materials, exporting nations, competitors and overseas markets.

Utilizing BI thus, corporations strive to achieve their strategic targets.

This calls for a system of BI collection and analysis, and for that system, we need strategies for linking and combining collected information and detecting trends. In this way, BI — highly value-added business information — becomes management tools to provide top management with intelligence and knowledge. Herbert E. Meyer predicts that such BI systems for collecting information will grow larger in scale and more efficient than national intelligence services.

Japanese corporations are said to be inferior to their European and American counterparts in their information analysis ability. They should therefore focus their efforts on enhancing their information analysis ability.

According to an intelligence specialist, almost 97% of necessary information can be obtained from public and open sources and from private sources. Therefore, it is not necessary to resort to unlawful means or spying. What is important here is not obtaining that mere 3% of secret information, which would infringe on corporate ethics and corporate governance, but ascertaining if the necessary information is securely gathered, if there is any redundant information, and whether or not the sources are reliable. In other words, what is important is "Information Audit."

In corporate accounting and financial audit, we examine if funds are properly used and whether any unlawful deeds are committed. Likewise, we should consider intelligence as capital and assets of corporations, and audit intelligence activities too. Here, it should be clearly noted that "information audit" is as important as accounting and financial audit for corporate management.

Herbert E. Meyer emphasizes that companies which can understand their own information environment and that of their competitors and establish competitive management strategies will win in this rapidly globalizing information society. He further predicts that BI and BI systems will revolutionize management tools.

The biggest weapon of corporations and organizations in the 21st century is "Intellectual Capital," which has not been fully developed yet. Intellectual capital consists of intelligence, knowledge and wisdom.

"Intellectual Capital" will become the new assets of companies to replace "machines," "financial capital," and "land" of the 20th century, and "intelligence" will become the major profit-generating factor in this century. Under such circumstances, it is imperative for companies to obtain value-added intelligence which translates to profits — that is to say, valuable business intelligence — in order to secure competitive advantages.

About 10,000 years ago during the Agricultural Age, the foundation of power was land. The Industrial Revolution transferred power to capital. However, the 21st century is the era of intelligence and knowledge; the source of power has shifted to intelligence, knowledge, education, intellectual ability, software and culture. Hence, education on intelligence and business intelligence in general is crucial in this era.

Information is classified into the following three categories:

(1) Public and open information;
(2) Private information;
(3) Confidential information.

In business, we must not deal with confidential information which would require espionage to obtain it. It is of utmost importance that we gather information ethically. An American organization, Society of Competitive Intelligence Professionals (SCIP), has a Code of Ethics emphasizing the importance of ethics in intelligence activities. The main objective of BI is obtaining competitive advantage by BI methods in areas such as business development, restructuring of corporations, strategic alliances, M&A, overseas investment, and risk management.

3. The Roles of Business Intelligence

The roles of business intelligence are:

(1) Deepening and expanding of existing business;
(2) Risk management;

(3) Information control, and security control and maintenance;
(4) Information manipulation.

That is to say, BI activities encompass all activities in collecting, analyzing and utilizing every kind of information including open, private, confidential, critical, aggressive, and defensive information; furthermore, primary and direct information, secondary and indirect information, human intelligence, documents, images, communications, competitive information, technology and patent information, and accounting and financial information.

To fulfill the above roles, the Chief Information Officer (CIO) and Chief Knowledge Officer (CKO) should conduct a thorough Information Audit, introducing the method of Supply Chain Management (SCM). It is recommended that Information Chain Management (ICM), Knowledge Chain Management (KCM) and Value Chain Management (VCM), which I am a proponent of, are effectively implemented.

The method of ICM is to refine and add value to information by linking target-setting and information, and by repeating the entire sequence of target-setting, information-gathering, selection, checking the sources, analysis, assessment, utilization, intelligence audit and review. The key is to link information of the past, present and future, and to have clear images of targets, so that the future can be predicted accurately. For multifaceted, multilateral and multilayered utilization of information, linking information — "correlation," "combination," and "collaboration" — becomes crucial.

Information does not lessen in value when given to others; in fact, information tends to accumulate when we offer it to others. To make use of this nature of information for effective information gathering, we need to first give before taking it. BI activities have to be done in the spirit of "give and take." This is what distinguishes information from other tangible things and products.

Undoubtedly, intelligence education, especially creative education, will become very important in the 21st century for government, industry and academia, in the rapidly globalized society where intelligence and knowledge rule. Today, 80% of computer databases are in

English. It is estimated that at least two billion people in the world can communicate in English. When 1.3 billion Chinese people communicate in English, the total number of English speakers will soar to some three billion; that is, almost half of the entire population of the world will be able to communicate in English.

The keywords of this century are information, English and international relations. To survive the 21st century, competency in English, interests in international relations, and BI abilities will become important assets for acquiring a competitive advantage.

Dr. Benjamin Gilad of Rutgers University notes that there is a flood of information in the world today, and yet, intelligence — truly useful, value-added information — is as scarce as water in the desert.

We must therefore study and learn BI, and become able to collect information, evaluate and analyze it, and add value to it, thus turning information into intelligence. To reiterate: if we are to survive in the fierce global competition of the new century, clearly we need Intelligence Education — education on information, ICT and intelligence.

Chapter 2

Competition and Intelligence

1. Competition and Business Intelligence

1.1. *Business intelligence is still not a familiar concept in Japan*

It is said that the term "business intelligence" was introduced in 1972 by the late Dr. Stevan Dedijer, professor at Lund University, Sweden. Dr. Dedijer had studied nuclear physics and had connections with the intelligence agencies in the US and Russia. In his later years, he founded a business intelligence course at the graduate school of Lund University. He was renowned amongst intelligence specialists as the authority on intelligence study.

Along with the former Vice Chairman of the National Intelligence Council, Mr. Herbert E. Meyer, Dr. Dedijer was critical of the trends in intelligence study in the US and Europe, which was focused on Competitive Intelligence (CI). (As someone who has studied competitive and business intelligence for over 20 years, I have to agree with the two specialists.)

It was only in 1988 that Gartner, headquartered in the US, started to promote Business Intelligence (BI). In recent years, IBM also has actively studied and used BI methods in connection with its Customer Relationship Management (CRM).

I established the Business Intelligence Society of Japan in 1992, and have been actively studying and promoting BI in Japan since then. Although the term "Business Intelligence" has gradually gained currency in Japan, compared to Europe and the US, BI is still far from being a popular, widespread concept in Japan.

1.2. *The era of competitive intelligence*

It was after the Society of Competitive Intelligence Professionals (SCIP) was established in the suburbs of Washington, D.C., Virginia in 1986, that the study of CI became active. The Society was established by those related to the US Intelligence agencies, and by government officials, scholars, and business people who were engaged in intelligence activities. The aim of SCIP is to study the methods employed by the CIA, the MI6, and the MOSSAD in information gathering, analysis, evaluation, and exploitation when confronting their intelligence competitors or virtual enemies, and to apply them to business to gain competitive advantage over competitors.

Dr. Prescott of the University of Pittsburgh defines CI as follows: "It can be applied to speed up and improve the quality of decision making. Intelligence helps make prospects or calculations when taking competitive actions."

On the other hand, Greene (1986) defines BI as "processed information which executives are extremely interested in, for such intelligence can influence companies' actions today and in the future." According to Ben Gilad, former Associate Professor at Rutgers University, BI is "information which is processed, analyzed, interpreted, and understood for the purpose of decision making."

Herbert E. Meyer defines BI in slightly different ways: "organized information for those decision makers," "information which helps companies make decisions in a proper timing and manner," and "analyzed information which is given to decision makers to satisfy their needs."

Furthermore, he asserts that companies need to construct BI systems for tracking raw material suppliers, supplying countries, competitors, customer growth, trends in overseas markets, as well as trends in areas related to their targets such as politics, economics, science and technology. It is his belief that corporate BI systems will, in future, grow larger in scale and be more efficient than the largest national intelligence system.

Just as Sir Francis Bacon — a British politician and philosopher — proclaimed that "knowledge is power" in 1620, we are currently facing an era when "intelligence" and "knowledge" mean power. Effective use of CI and BI is now essential for corporate survival in this knowledge society of the 21st century.

In such an era, there is an urgent need for Japanese corporations to study CI and BI, and make use of it to acquire competitive advantages in the fierce global competition of the new era.

2. Competitive Intelligence and Business Intelligence

2.1. *Dr. Dedijer's theory*

While CI was at the center of intelligence study in Europe and the US, Dr. Dedijer believed that more focus should be given to BI. In his view, CI merely formed part of BI.

Dr. Dedijer referred to the Catholic Church, the British Empire, and the Bank of Switzerland as perfect examples of intelligence agencies which had outstanding intelligence abilities. He therefore insisted that we should study these three organizations as pioneers of intelligence activities. He also highly regarded "C&C" (Computer and Communication) theory as advocated by Mr. Kobayashi, former NEC chairman.

Dr. Dedijer divided BI into two genres: Business I (intelligence for pursuit of profits for individuals, social systems, and corporations) and Business II (intelligence for all other purposes). He insisted that to acquire Business I, we must adapt to the changing environment and learn to utilize ability, knowledge, individual talents, and social systems, while making use of science. Characteristically, his study's main focus was on both intelligence and security.

2.2. *History of intelligence*

Dr. Dedijer notes that the human race has been engaged in intelligence activities for over 5,000 years; there is evidence that early rulers and merchants used what was called "Organized Intelligence." In the Middle Ages — the era of craftsmanship and mercantilism — the concept of BI first appeared in the Latin expression, "*intelligentia pecunaie querendo*" (intelligence for gaining money). Such intelligence was systematically used by the Fuggers in 15th century Germany, by the Medicis in 16th and 17th century Italy, by the Rothschilds in 19th century Europe, and by the Warenbergs in 20th century Sweden.

According to the autobiography of T. Browald, president of Handelsbank, what enabled Catholic churches since the 5th century, the British Empire since 1600, and Swedish banks since 1800 to prosper and survive over many years was that they all possessed top-class organized intelligence.

In 1600, a British writer, R. Hakluyt, drew up 700 reports on Economic Intelligence and became a consultant to the East India Company. In 1995, F. MacLean established an economic intelligence company called "Hakluyt Co." Meanwhile, in 1919, Sir Winston Churchill established an industrial intelligence section within his Cabinet. Since 1936, this industrial intelligence section has become part of the Central Office of Intelligence (COI) in the UK.

Even before 1945 and during the Cold War, from the British Empire to the USSR, all empires utilized intelligence. According to Dr. Dedijer, the first description of military intelligence was found in *The Art of War*, a book written by Sun Tzu in the 5th century BC in China. As for political intelligence, Kayutilla of India and Aristotle of Greece, among others, made distinctions between information, knowledge, and intelligence.

In 180 BC, Plato shared his insight in his *To Intelligent Persons*, that intelligence means effective use of information systems. Dr. Dedijer, however, states that intelligence is a systematic problem-solving process: recognizing and analyzing problems, converting information into intelligence, thus solving problems.

2.3. *Competitive intelligence and business intelligence*

a. *CI is insufficient on its own*

Established in 1986 in the US, SCIP now has over 3,000 members and it has held intelligence conferences not only within the US but also in Europe. An annual international conference on CI is held every year within the US, and more than 1,000 intelligence specialists attend research presentations and workshops.

As mentioned earlier, Dr. Dedijer, one of the top business intelligence researchers, was critical of the research method which focused solely on collecting information about competitors.

Mr. H. E. Meyer, former Vice Chairman of the National Intelligence Council, also found CI-oriented research problematic. In his book, *Real-World Intelligence* (translated into Japanese by Juro Nakagawa), he clearly points out: "it is without doubt that competitive intelligence is becoming the mainstream among American companies." He says that focusing on CI is just the first step in the long process of developing intelligence systems, which are more effective and broader in scope. He warns that although it is important to know what your competitors are up to, that alone is not enough.

In the recent high-tech business environment, companies that would cause great damage to themselves were not even considered as competitors. For example, a major typewriter company with a top-class CI system would have been aware of what its rivals were up to. Nevertheless, it would receive a vital blow from two young fellows who invented personal computers in their garage in the Silicon Valley.

Thus, problems may arise if you focus solely on existing competitors. What is important is to have a general view of various influences that are working on competitors in the prevailing economic situation.

Meyer emphasizes that although it is necessary to study competitors, it is even more important to recognize and oversee clients' progress, overseas market trends, and political, economic, scientific, and technical trends; and, moreover, to convey such intelligence to top management to aid in their corporate strategy decision-making.

b. *Intelligence strategy of a Japanese trading company*

A manager of one of the major Japanese trading companies which I profiled says that collaboration is more important than competition, and that "Competitive Intelligence" is a term rarely heard in his office.

This prestigious trading company, with its 150 years of history, has 650 group businesses within and outside of Japan, hires 60,000 employees, and has seven in-house companies. The main company has 4,122 employees, with 50 executive officers overlooking 17 domestic and 133 overseas branches. They utilize their network of over 6,000 retailers and distributors to collect, share and integrate information; this "Decision Support System" (DSS) contributes to decision-making at the management level.

The company, however, has never paid attention to the concept of "competitive intelligence," as it has been conducting business on a "win-win" basis. Even competing companies may become partners. Therefore, they seek general economic information for business, or business intelligence, from such sources as the United Nations statistics, the World Bank, the IMF, OECD, the Fortune 500, research companies, investment funds, and venture capital firms, among others.

Researchers reporting directly to the president, staff in the president's office, and executive officers in charge of management planning analyze the gathered information, add value to it, and report it as decision-making intelligence to the president. This intelligence is then managed by the Systems Planning Department and the CIO in the information system. Representatives of the seven in-house companies gather once a week to share information.

According to the manager of the Information Research Division whom I interviewed, it is difficult to share all the relevant information to 50 executive officers; therefore, it is important to clarify the objective and to specify the range of information. The number of staff in charge of intelligence in this company is about 5% of the total number of employees.

c. *Intelligence strategy of IBM*

According to Mr. Narita, BI officer at IBM Japan, IBM makes use of BI especially in Customer Relationship Management (CRM). In other words, BI is used to secure good customers.

IBM has watched over changes in its customers particularly closely since the burst of the bubble economy in the 1990s. Following the 80/20 Rule, its strategies of securing customers place a special emphasis on customer lifetime value; the company utilizes BI in its customer-oriented strategies of analyzing customer data, penetrating deeper into existing customers, and obtaining a competitive edge.

Through BI, IBM reinforces business process knowledge, product and service knowledge, and market knowledge, using knowledge management methods. It attempts to share, internalize, and systematize BI, and through Group Ware Data Warehouse and Data Mining, optimizes analysis by multi-dimensional analysis, statistical analysis, complex data query and so on. In this, analysis of time-series patterns and data analysis are important, and so is finding the unknown rules in correlations. IBM believes that this is crucial to enhance companies' changing and learning capacity.

In order to implement strategies as a global company, it is important to collect, integrate and process BI, and to feed it back to the workforce at the front. Mr. Narita emphasizes that BI should serve as a cockpit for managing the company.

d. *Professor Akihiro Okumura's IT strategic theory*

Professor Akihiro Okumura of Keio University is engaged in research on INCS, Inc., the manufacturer famous for IT-driven design and production of molds. He asserts that personnel management and adding value to R&D and Marketing are keys to obtaining competitive advantages through knowledge management. He insists that Japanese manufacturers' competitive advantages should be turned into "knowledge" by IT, that companies should renovate themselves and win the "software race." For this to happen, he says that R&D and Marketing departments should be added value to, in order to maintain their competitive edge, and that the production base should be transferred overseas. A similar idea was mentioned in the *2007 JETRO White Paper on Trade and Investment.*

INCS, Inc., the leading IT company among 7,000 mold-and-die manufacturers in Japan, whose share is 44% of the world market, has developed revolutionary software which spirals tacit knowledge into formal knowledge, by connecting IT, computers, intelligence and knowledge with people. The company connects intelligence and knowledge with people through introducing IT and knowledge management into the manufacturing industry, thereby enhancing its competitiveness on a win-win basis.

The strategy for surviving the global competition is to turn Japanese manufacturers' employees into "Knowledge Workers." Japanese car makers use 30,000 press dies in their 3,000 processes. Therefore, knowledge management is vital for design and production of these press dies for Japan's competitive edge. Professor Okumura also believes that knowledge and intelligence, which creates value out of the intangible, is the key to Japan's future; use of BI is crucial for obtaining competitive advantages.

e. *The current state of business intelligence*

According to Gartner's report for the Gartner Business Intelligence Summit that was held in Tokyo in February 2007, it is evident that some positive results can be seen after BI was introduced to the company. Specifically, speed-up in decision-making, improvement in productivity, and streamlining of business processes were graded 3 out of 5.

Cut-down on operational cost, going paperless, and obtaining competitive advantage scored between 2.5 to 3. Not much effect was noted in sales increase, improvement in customer satisfaction, and acquiring new customers, whose scores were around 2.5. Some issues regarding the use of BI were pointed out: lack of users' and technicians' skills, unclear cost-performance, high system introduction cost, low frequency of use, lack of organization of data, and absence of an analysis department. For successful use of BI, multiple skills are necessary, such as business skills, IT skills, and analysis skills.

It is important to build BI infrastructure, for example, data integration in the IT department under the supervision of the CIO; to establish a Business Intelligence Competency Center (BICC) under the CFO, which is in charge of promotion, development and maintenance; and to gain the trust of other departments by holding regular meetings.

f. *Competitive strategy of INCS*

INCS, Inc., is a major IT knowledge-based company. As part of its competitive and differentiated strategies, the company hires 1,400 "knowledge workers." Aiming to become a 3D-CAD-based molding and development consultant, the company uses IT in new product development, and has built value chains from the planning stage, design, trial products, experiments, and mass production, to manufacturing, in its attempt to create business opportunities. By developing innovative technologies, it has achieved dramatic cost-down, nifty management, and market-based product development; the company has also upgraded its business model by using IT, and has established a new business model for manufacturers by making good use of knowledge links. Thus, INCS has acquired innovative competitive abilities; it introduced 27 SLA, which is second to GM, and cut down the time it took to manufacture molding prototypes of cellular phones from 48 days to 48 hours.

g. *Google's intelligence strategies*

Google, a rapidly growing 21st-century IT company, is like an "intelligence powerhouse." Its intelligence strategies are similar to those of INCS — gather outstanding personnel; provide a creative, liberal and open environment; share information completely among all staff members; attach great importance to swiftness; and promote keen competition within the corporation.

This is different from competitive intelligence strategy, which concentrates solely on gathering and analyzing information relating to external competitors. Business intelligence values competition within the organization as well, in its attempt to gain competitive advantage. This is the direction we should follow.

h. *Dr. Kenichi Ohmae's intelligence strategy theory*

Dr. Kenichi Ohmae states in his recent book, *Ken Ohmae on Strategy*:

> "To win against your rival is not the primary subject. It surely is not wrong to have competitive advantage in production capability,

product development, and logistics; however, it is not strategy's object itself — nor should it be. If you are determined to beat your rivals at whatever cost, your strategies will change constantly depending on what steps your competitors take.

What we must consider first is customers' needs. Strategy should be customer-oriented. You can think about beating your rivals after you establish your strategy. What should come first, before anything else, is strategy that creates customer value."

This notion of Ohmae's is in line with not only the ideas of Dr. Dedijer and Mr. H. E. Meyer, but also that of Toyota and INCS.

3. Security and Confidentiality Issues

3.1. *The US strategy for intelligence security*

Dr. Dedijer focuses on business creation and security of critical information when discussing BI's roles. In 1976, he taught a class on "Security of industrial intelligence and spying" in his "Social Intelligence" course at Lund University, Sweden, which shows the importance he placed on confidentiality.

On May 10, 2001, Japanese intelligence specialists witnessed a shocking incident. The FBI prosecuted and arrested a Japanese chemist at Cleveland Clinic Institute over the theft of the Alzheimer's disease research materials, based on the Economic Espionage Act. They also prosecuted another chemist who had returned to Japan and requested his extradition.

The US enacted the "Economic Espionage Act" in October 1996, a pro-patent strategy to protect the confidentiality and security of forefront technologies (such as IT and biology) and business intelligence. Under this law, those individuals who engage in economic espionage could be fined $500,000 and/or sentenced to 15 years' imprisonment; for companies and institutions, the fine could be as high as $10 million.

The Economic Espionage Act covers diverse areas such as corporate confidentiality, high technology, patents, and intellectual property rights. For this reason, great care must be taken when collecting information in the US.

Knowledge and information — such as information technology, biotechnology, and intellectual property rights — will be the driving force of the 21st century. In the global corporate war, information, technology and intellectual property rights will be the main battlefield. Especially in Asian countries such as China, Korea, Taiwan, and Hong Kong, cases of counterfeit products and infringement on trademarks and intellectual property rights are frequent occurrences. Indeed, the US has brought several such complaints against China to the WTO, in order to settle the dispute.

Under such circumstances, therefore, it is imperative to study the Economic Espionage Act thoroughly and take appropriate countermeasures.

3.2. *Economic Espionage Act of 1996*

To avoid getting embroiled in espionage disputes with the US, let us take a quick glance at the Economic Espionage Act. Article 1831 states that it is against the law, "intending or knowing that the offense will benefit any foreign government, foreign instrumentality, or foreign agent, knowingly —":

(1) to steal, or without authorization appropriate, take, carry away, or conceal, or by fraud, artifice, or deception obtain a trade secret;
(2) to without authorization copy, duplicate, sketch, draw, photograph, download, upload, alter, destroy, photocopy, replicate, transmit, deliver, send, mail, communicate, or convey a trade secret;
(3) to receive, buy, or possess a trade secret, knowing the same to have been stolen or appropriated, obtained, or converted without authorization.

Article 1832 states that it is a crime to commit the above deeds knowingly, "with intent to convert a trade secret, that is related to or included in a product that is produced for or placed in interstate or foreign commerce, to the economic benefit of anyone other than the owner thereof, and intending or knowing that the offense will injure any owner of that trade secret."

Asian and Japanese governments, research institutions, and corporations must be extremely cautious when conducting intelligence-related activities in the US. In addition, Japan should establish a similarly stringent law to protect the security of its own corporate intelligence.

4. Echelon — the International Communications Surveillance System

The European Parliament set up a temporary committee to investigate the global surveillance system, Echelon, and published its final report on May 18, 2001. That report, which the European Parliament approved, contained some shocking findings.

Echelon is a global communications surveillance system which is mainly used by the National Security Agency (NSA), and also by four other nations including the UK, Canada, Australia and New Zealand, to intercept, analyze and process telecommunications, fax, and email all over the world. The word "Echelon" is a code that means "a ladder."

The 113-page investigation report, which took the committee nearly one year to draft, revealed the existence of a global signals intelligence system (i.e., Echelon), led by the US, so far mysteriously shrouded in national security. Echelon has caused serious human rights violations such as infringement on privacy, and monitoring and tapping of private communication.

Asian countries should cooperate with the EU countries to regulate intelligence activities and to raise this issue on a global scale. Also, relevant governments should be aware of the fact that their important communications may be monitored. Every caution should be taken with communications, and it is desirable to use codes and ciphers.

There are 20 suspected monitoring stations in the world, including those in Guam, Hong Kong (closed down in 1994), New Zealand, Australia, and Misawa US Air Base in Aomori, Japan.

After the Cold War, intelligence agencies shifted their target from military intelligence to economic and technology information, aiming for supremacy in the economic sphere. An economic intelligence war has already begun all around the world. The European Parliament's investigation report revealed the reality of this, and Asian and other countries should become alert to it. To caution the world, the report gives specific examples of 28 major cases of intercepting and tapping in the global market.

The following are examples of various cases that Duncan Campbell, the journalist who conducted the investigation, disclosed in the investigation report. One such case pertaining to Asia was when the CIA broke into the computers of the Japanese Ministry of International Trade and Industry and passed on the information obtained to the then US Trade Representative, Michael Kantor, in time for the trade negotiations on the Japanese import quota for American cars in 1996. The report also revealed another case of America's illegal interception of information relating to exhaust gas regulation for Japanese high-end cars.

During the international tender for Korea's high-speed rail cars, GEC/Alsthom (the UK-French alliance) stole bidding information from AEG/Siemens, which was originally considered to be the favored candidate, and ended up winning the contract.

A similar case was when the Boeing Company and McDonnell Douglas monitored and intercepted Airbus S.A.S's satellite communications via facsimile and telephone in an aircraft sales competition, and stole the six-billion-dollar deal with Saudi Arabia from Airbus S.A.S. The American side criticized Airbus of committing bribery, proof of which was obtained from the illegal interception of their competitor's communications.

The above demonstrates that, especially during important international business negotiations, the relevant corporations must make thorough preparations to protect their confidential information. This is vital for Asian corporations to survive the international business war, which is becoming ever fiercer.

5. Case Studies

5.1. *Asian economic crisis and intelligence strategy*

Almost 60% of Japanese corporations that invested in and were engaged in business in Asia were affected by the Asian economic crisis on July 2, 1997. Less than 10% was not affected or made some profits (JETRO). What is notable here is that 80% of those corporations that were negatively affected by the crisis lost profit due to poor risk management.

The study of risk management started with the management policy study in Germany in the 1920s. The term "risk management," however, is comparatively new; it only gained currency in Japan during the 1950s.

In the 1970s, Ataka & Co., Ltd., a Japanese general trading company with a century's worth of prestigious history, disappeared from the business scene as it had lost 100 billion yen on oil refinery projects in Come By Chance, Canada. In the 1970s and 1980s, Mitsui & Co., Ltd., one of the leading general trading companies in Japan, made a loss of 400 billion yen on its petrochemical project in Iran. Furthermore, Sumitomo Corporation lost 280 billion yen in the speculative transaction of copper from 1993 to 1994 — all of which highlighted the need for the study of risk management.

The main cause of the Asian economic crisis is considered to be the sudden and acute fluctuation in foreign exchange rates, which carried inevitable risk. Nevertheless, Mitsui was successful in controlling this risk during the monetary crisis in Thailand. Upon close examination of this case, it can be seen that Mitsui's Bangkok branch office had an advanced, competitive risk management system: gathering risk information, controlling risk by early warning system, sharing information, and crises management. Based on analysis of the intelligence collected, Mitsui had anticipated and foreseen the baht crisis in advance and hedged 100% of the exchange risk against US dollars. Mitsui had thus constructed a company-wide

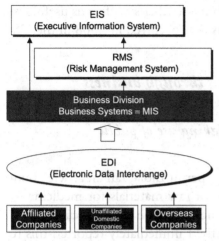

1) EIS (Executive Information System)
To disseminate information to the top
management to contribute to their decision
making;
   * on planning and policy making
   * on investment
   * on affiliated companies' management
   * on positioning
   * on various macro-information
   * on government offices and authorities

2) RMS (Risk Management System)
For countermeasures to deal and cope with
various risk systems;
   * Enterprise and business risks (Affiliated
   companies and new venture business)
   * Credit risks (Counterparty risks, country
   risks)
   * Market risks (Merchandise, Foreign
   Exchange and Interest Rate fluctuation risks)
   * Merchandise risks (Stocks, Inventory risks)
   * System risks (Disasters, Accidents, Crimes)

Figure 2:   Japanese Trading Company's Information System

Source: M-Trading Company's data.

intelligence system consisting of an Executive Information System
(EIS) — a system that offers support for decision-making by executives — and a Risk Management System (RMS) — a system
that manages risk in business, credit, markets, products and systems
(see Figure 2).

RMS detects where business risk lies among affiliated companies
and new businesses, and where credit risk lies among counterparts
and countries. For market risk, RMS analyzes fluctuations in product
prices and foreign exchange rates. Product risk involves inventory risk
management, while system risk, importantly, is about contingencies
such as accidents and crimes, and about managing risk factors.

Mitsui avoided the Thai monetary crisis and even recorded profits
at the time, by analyzing the information collected by its 7,000 computers in Japan and 5,000 computers overseas. Mitsui's success can be
compared to that of the major multinational corporation, Royal
Dutch Shell, in predicting the 1973 oil shock and the financial collapse of the USSR during the 1990s, and then profiting from them
by making full use of its intelligence.

Mitsui's method of dealing with financial crisis offers us useful lessons for the subprime financial crisis that occurred in 2008 in the US.

5.2. *Creating new businesses through business intelligence*

a. *Pharmaceutical products (Making use of public information — newspaper)*

Hindustan Times, an English newspaper in India, ran an article about the news that there was a shortage of raw materials for medicine — specifically, antibiotics — and that the Indian pharmaceutical industry and medical care would suffer greatly. I immediately reported this to Japan and persuaded a pharmaceutical company to provide raw materials for penicillin, streptomycin, and vitamin A. After some tough negotiations with the State Trading Corporation of India, I succeeded in exporting a great amount of raw materials for drugs from Japan to India for the first time. This business has since continued for many years. This case study therefore shows that it is possible to create a new big business even from a piece of information in a newspaper article.

b. *Car export (Critical intelligence from human sources — HUMINT)*

I had obtained information from a counterpart in Rio de Janeiro, Brazil, that Chile would be lifting the ban on car imports shortly. Normally, this is as much as one would hear from a source. However, this source provided me with further critical information, which allowed me to obtain a large export contract of 40,000 cars (approximately 50 billion yen) over other competitors.

The critical information was that the import duty would be 100% for cars with under 1000cc engines, but it would be 200% for cars with over 1000cc engines, in order to curb gasoline consumption. I immediately cabled this top-secret information to Japan. Consequently, cars with 800cc engines were offered, and we won the first big orders for car imports from South America. This business also has continued for many years. It is therefore extremely important to make efforts to improve BI, so that we can make use of critical intelligence for business immediately.

6. Conclusion — Japan Must Focus on BI and Intelligence Education

As we have seen, BI is critical not only for deepening and expanding existing businesses and creating and developing new businesses, but also for risk management, intelligence security, knowledge management, intellectual property business, and business in frontier technologies such as biotechnology and nanotechnology industries.

In this era of information and globalization, the importance of intelligence is increasing, and intelligence education, especially at the university level, is vital. BI has become an indispensable tool to secure competitive advantage, as competition becomes ever fiercer on a global scale.

In recent years, intelligence education has become quite active in universities and graduate schools, especially in Sweden, the US, Canada, France, and most recently in China. Of particular note are intelligence war academies in the US, Sweden, and France, and also Ecole Européenne d'Intelligence Economique (EEIE), which was established in Versailles in September 2006 (for further details, please refer to Chapter 6, Section 3). We should also pay close attention to CI education at the Academy of Competitive Intelligence in Boston, USA (for further details, please refer to Chapter 3, Section 3, and Chapter 6, Section 2).

References

Dedijer, Stevan, "Microsoft's Intelligence & Security Doctrine", Conference Intelligence Economique et Concurrentielle, Paris, June 1999.

Dedijer, Stevan, "What I learned from 1972 to 2000 about Business Intelligence", Prepared for the IBM, Sweden e-Commerce Conference, April 5, 2000.

Gilad, Ben and Tamal Gilad, Translated by Juro Nakagawa *et al.*, [*Global kigyo no Joho Sosiki Senryaku*] *Business Intelligence System*, Eruko, 1996.

Iida, Takeo, [*Kakusite kyoudai Sonshutuwa Kaigaide Umareta*] *Big Loss in Overseas Business was Thus Made*, Nippon Hyoronsha, November 1998.

Iwashima, Y., [*Leader to Joho-ryoku*] *Leader and Intelligence Power*, Satsuki Shobo, May 2002.

JETRO White Paper on Trade and Investment 2007, September 2007.

Kamei, Toshiaki, [*Kiki kanri to risk manejimento*] *Crisis and Risk Management*, Dobunkan, 1997.

Kuroiwa, Buntaro, [*Nippon no Johokikan*] *Japanese Intelligence Agency*, Kodansha, September 2007.

Meyer, H.E., Translated by Juro Nakagawa *et al.*, [*CIA ryu Senryaku Joho Tokuhon*] *Real-World Intelligence*, Diamond Publishing, 1990.

Miyazaki, T., [*kigyo Joho wa Konna Tede Nusumareru*] *How the Corporate Secret Information Has Been Stolen*, Toyo Keizai Shimposha, January 2005.

Nakagawa, Juro *et al.*, *The Intelligent Corporation*, Taylor Graham, London, UK, 1992.

Nakagawa, Juro, [*Boekishosha ni okeru Joho no Yakuwari*] "The role of information in a Japanese Trading Company", Nihon Boekigakkai Nenpo-Japanese Academy of International Business and Foreign Trade — Annual Report, 1993.

Nakagawa, Juro *et al.*, *The Global Perspectives of Competitive Intelligence*, SCIP, Virginia, USA, 1993.

Nakagawa, Juro, [*Kokusai Marketing ni okeru Risk bunsekito Risk kanrini kansuru Ichikosatu*] *A Study on Risk Analysis and Risk Management in International Marketing*, Aichi Gakuin University (Chiiki Bunseki), December 1994.

Nakagawa, Juro, [*Business Kyogojoho no Kenkyu*] *A Study on Business and Competitive Intelligence*, Aichi Gakuin University (Ryutu Kenkyu), March 1995.

Nakagawa, Juro, [*Beikoku Spy Boshiho ga Imisurumono*] "The meaning of Economic Espionage Act of the USA", *Weekly Toyo Keizai Shimpo*, September 18, 1997.

Nakagawa, Juro, [*Kokusai Budaide Kigyono ikinokorio Kimeru CIA ryu Joho Senryakutowa Nanika*] *Intelligence Strategy of CIA to Make Corporations Survive in Severe International Competition*, Takarajimasha, 2000.

Nakagawa, Juro, [*Ajia Keizaikiki to Joho Senryaku*] "Intelligence Strategy in Asian Economic Crisis", *Asian Club Annual Report*, 2000.

Nakagawa, Juro, [*Chiteki Shoyuken Funso to Beikoku Keizai Spy Hoo*] "Intellectual Property dispute and U.S.A. Economic Espionage Act", *Asia Club Monthly*, July 2001.

Nakagawa, Juro, [*Gekka suru Keizai Joho Senso — Echelon Bocho System no Jittai*] "Intensifying Economic Intelligence War — the real situation of Echelon's illegal listening system", *Asia Club Monthly*, No. 50, August 2001.

Nakagawa, Juro, [*Risk manejimento to Joho Senryaku*] "Risk Management and Information Strategy", Japanese Academy of International Business and Foreign Trade — Annual Report, March 2003.

Ohmae, Kenichi, [*Ohmae Kenichi Senryakuron*] *Ken Ohmae on Strategy*, Diamond Publishing, October 2007.

Okazaki, Hisahiko, [*Nihon Gaiko no Juho Senryaku*] *Japanese Diplomacy Intelligence Strategy*, PHP, March 2003.

Rapp, William, Translated by Juro Nakagawa *et al.*, [*Seiko kigyono IT Senryaku*] *Information Technology Strategy*, Nikkei BP, 2003.

Saito, Yoshio, Juro Nakagawa *et al.*, [*Kokusai Keiei Senryaku*] *International Business Management Strategy*, Dobunkan, 1996.

Sato, Suguru *et al.*, [*Kokka Joho Senryaku*] *National Intelligence Strategy*, Kodansha, July 2007.

Tejima, Ryuichi and Suguru Sato, [*Intelligence bukinaki senso*] *War without Weapons*, Gentosha, November 2006.

Tuchiya, T., [*Netto Waaku Power*] *Network Power*, NTT, January 2007.

Umeda, N., [*Web Shinkaron*] *The Theory of Web Evolution*, Chikuma Shobo, February 2006.

Chapter 3

Business and Competitive Intelligence Strategy in the Age of Informatization

1. Privatization of Intelligence

Since the end of the Cold War in 1989, intelligence agencies in the world have shifted the focus of their activities from collecting military intelligence to collecting economic and business intelligence. This is the so-called "privatization of intelligence" (Dr. Stevan Dedijer of Lund University, Sweden).

Before the end of the Cold War, the Society of Competitive Intelligence Professionals (SCIP) was established in Virginia, the suburbs of Washington, D.C. in 1986, by intelligence experts including CIA and military intelligence officers from the US intelligence community whose budget was estimated to be around $45 billion at the time.

The SCIP currently has about 3,000 members from all over the world, and it has become one of the largest CI research institutes in the world. Under the Clinton administration, with the introduction of strategies for National Information Infrastructure (NII), Global Information Infrastructure (GII), and Information and Communication Technology (ICT), and with a shift in the national policy from the "Nuclear Umbrella" to the "Information Umbrella," the study of business and competitive intelligence showed remarkable progress in the 1990s.

Today, most Fortune 500 corporations have intelligence professionals who apply their knowledge of military intelligence technology to business and strive to gain competitive advantage, making full use of

ICT and the Internet, in this era of economic intelligence war. Truly, "those who control intelligence control the business" nowadays.

As already mentioned, the Clinton administration enacted the Economic Espionage Act (EEA) in 1996, in protection of intelligence and intellectual property. This Act imposes severe penalties on people and foreign corporations that have stolen secret corporate information illegally (for further details, refer to Chapter 2, Section 3, and Chapter 5, Section 1). The aforementioned case of a Japanese chemist at the Cleveland Clinic Institute who was charged with theft of the Alzheimer's disease research materials was based on the EEA.

Economic intelligence war schools have been established in the US, France and Sweden. At these schools, students are trained to become intelligence experts.

Then there is the formidable Echelon, the largest intelligence surveillance system in the world, whose existence was recently revealed. It is operated by five nations (the US, the UK, Canada, Australia and New Zealand). The EU Parliament has criticized Echelon as a spying network that illegally collects economic intelligence, not just military information, from all over the world.

In Asia, we have the Business Intelligence Society of Japan, which I founded in 1992. The Business Intelligence Society of Japan has held study meetings every other month for the past 18 years. In addition, societies of CI professionals were established in 1993 in Australia and China, where CI study is more active than in Japan. Recently, Singapore has also established an intelligence society.

As I mentioned earlier, the US, the UK, France and Sweden are actively studying CI to prepare for the international economic intelligence war in the 21st century. In response, Japan should take the initiative in forming an Asian Business Intelligence Society that includes countries such as China, Korea, Singapore, and India.

2. World Trends in Business and Competitive Intelligence Study

As mentioned earlier, the study of business and competitive intelligence truly began when the Society of Competitive Intelligence

Professionals (SCIP) was established in Virginia, USA in 1986. I first became involved with the society 20 years ago, when the Japan External Trade Organization (JETRO) asked me to give a speech titled "The Collection of Business Information and Development of Global Business in the Japanese General Trading Company" (*"sogo-shosha"* in Japanese) at the SCIP New York Meeting in 1989, when I was Vice President of Business Development at Nichimen America Inc., New York.

It was at this conference that I met Dr. Benjamin Gilad, who was also invited as a speaker. This led to my translating Dr. Gilad's book, *Business Intelligence Systems*, in 1996.

Since the end of the Cold War in 1989, after the fall of the Berlin Wall, the world market has become borderless and globalized, and competition in the global market has severely intensified. The US and European countries therefore started to study CI eagerly, in order to obtain competitive advantage in the global market. As mentioned earlier, business and competitive intelligence study began in the UK, France, Belgium, Sweden, and Japan in 1992, and in Australia and China in 1993.

In 2002 I attended the SCIP annual conference in Cincinnati, where many stimulating speeches were given and serious discussions were held. I was amazed to see how advanced and active CI study had become in the US and Europe. The following are the topics of presentations and discussions at the conference:

- How to collect information at meetings
- How to develop a world-class market intelligence gathering process
- CI strategy for succeeding in today's business environment
- CI and market research
- CI — how to develop sales strategy and the market on the front lines
- CI and how to approach internal benchmarks
- CI for developing new business
- Strategic alliance between the Department of Competitive Intelligence and the Legal Department

- How to combine intelligence with strategy
- The process of analysis and integration of information
- CI and corporate intranet
- CI and knowledge management
- Combining value chain opportunities
- Intelligence technologies for CI
- Industry analysis by CI
- Strategic intelligence auditing
- Global CI — collection and analysis
- High Tech and CI
- High-speed information processing.

3. The Forefront of CI Education

In regards to CI, Japan is well behind US and UK corporations, their governments, and academia. Therefore, Japan should make every effort to further its study of information collection, analysis and utilization, to catch up with the US and the UK. Otherwise, Japanese companies will not be able to cope with their American and European competitors in the severe global competition climate.

The Academy of Competitive Intelligence (ACI) teaches students that early warning is vital for corporate survival. ACI is run by Mr. Leonard M. Fuld, President of Fuld & Company; Dr. Benjamin Gilad, former Associate Professor of Strategy at Rutgers University's Graduate School of Management; and Mr. Jan Herring, former Director of Intelligence at Motorola Inc., and former CIA officer.

In this academy, mainly executives and managers of Fortune 500 companies study the nine courses below, so that they can better cope with the economic intelligence war of this informatization era. The courses are taught by prominent intelligence experts, lawyers, and professors from Harvard University. Japan should take note of what they do at this academy.

The nine major courses are as follows:

- Course 1: Intelligence Sources & Collection Techniques
- Course 2: Competitive Benchmarking & Tactical Analysis

- Course 3: Competitive Blindspots
- Course 4: Cross-Competitor Analysis
- Course 5: Managing the Intelligence Program
- Course 6: War Gaming: Theory & Practice
- Course 7: Value Chain Analysis
- Course 8: Financial Issues
- Course 9: Ethical Boundary

It is also worthwhile to study the curriculum of the CI course at Pittsburgh University's Graduate School of Business, taught by Professor Prescott, which is considered to be one of the most advanced courses on CI. In this practice-oriented course, he teaches how to collect, analyze, utilize, combine and integrate information and intelligence for effective action. There is an emphasis on how to translate intelligence into action, and students learn how to design effective CI programs.

Thus, through this way, the military, the government, business and academia collaborate in business and competitive intelligence study in the US and Europe, preparing for the age of mega-competition in the globalized, information society of the 21st century.

Walmart heavily invested in constructing a large-scale intelligence system, and succeeded in achieving No. 1 sales in the world. Similarly, Itoh Yokado invested in information systems before any other company did, and became one of the leading retailers in Japan. Both companies are perfect examples of how good information strategy can lead to success.

In order to survive this century, it is imperative not only to construct information systems, but also to educate and train employees in BI. Furthermore, business, the government, and academia must cooperate in research and training of intelligence software for BI. Otherwise, Japan will inevitably lose the intelligence war in this era of informatization, just as it lost the finance war in the 1990s.

Chapter 4

CIA-Style Intelligence Strategy

After the Cold War ended, the wall between the Communist camp and the West came crumbling down. Consequently, the international market effective demand expanded from the previous one billion to three billion consumers, bringing on the era of mega-competition. In order to maintain a competitive edge in the global markets, closely linked by information networks, it is vital to have intelligence strategies for gathering and leveraging information.

Among the Directors of the Central Intelligence Agency (CIA), the first to recognize the importance of economic intelligence is said to be Stansfield M. Turner, who was appointed as Director of the CIA during the Carter administration. Turner predicted the coming of the era of an Intelligence War, when economic intelligence, rather than defense or military information, would be paramount for national defense and security. Since then, not only France and Germany but also China and Russia have come to consider it a national policy to gather information concerning technology, economy and industry. As the Internet has made a mass of information freely available online, we are now in the very midst of an Intelligence War.

For business management in this information-driven society, development of business intelligence and competitive intelligence systems will be the key for corporate survival. "Competitive intelligence" is a recent addition to the business lexicon in Japan; it is the private sector's attempt to adopt the techniques of world intelligence agencies, especially its most prominent example, the CIA, in gathering and analyzing information about rival nations.

1. Intelligence Analysis and Survival of Corporations

1.1. *Competitive Intelligence strategies in Europe and the United States*

In the United States, the Society of Competitive Intelligence Professionals (now the Strategic and Competitive Intelligence Professionals, or SCIP) was founded in 1986, with the aim of applying CIA-style information gathering and analysis techniques to business. Intelligence specialists from intelligence agencies, academia, business, and think-tanks played a principal role in the establishment of this organization. Currently, the SCIP has about 3,000 members from over 45 countries. This number includes many intelligence officials from the CIA and the Pentagon who joined the organization after the Cold War ended.

As evident from the fact that SCIP originally stood for "Society of Competitive Intelligence Professionals," its main objectives are to gather information about competitors, and to study how that information can be utilized for management strategies.

In the UK, the Association of Global Strategic Information (AGSI) was founded in 1992 and has been actively engaged in research since then. Meanwhile, in Switzerland, the Global Business Development Alliance (GBDA) was founded in 1996. It began research on development of global business through the use of BI and international networks of connections.

Australia and China have embarked on CI research, too. Incidentally, the Association of Competitive Intelligence of China was founded in 1995 by a network of over 400 research institutes that carry 20,000 members under the Institute of Scientific and Technical Information of China. These research institutes are all working to utilize intelligence for business.

2. Changing Business Intelligence Environment

2.1. *Vital information audit*

According to CIA officials, almost 97% of necessary information can be procured from public and private sources. It should be noted here that there is no need for illegal activities or espionage for gathering BI.

Rather than trying to obtain that last 3% of secret information, what is more important is ascertaining that the necessary information is gained and that there is no redundant information, i.e., Information Audit. H. E. Meyer argued in the 1990s that the BI system is an innovative system that will drastically transform business management. Solid auditing of data and information that create the "information flow" of the 21st century, and enhancement of information analytical power are the biggest factors that generate profits.

2.2. *Competitive Intelligence research by the SCIP*

Over 1,000 information professionals gather from all over the world at the annual international conventions of the SCIP. For reference, below are the categories for workshops at the Chicago convention (see also reports of the Cincinnati convention in Chapter 3 and the Orlando convention in Chapter 6):

- Techniques to uncover overseas and domestic competitors' secrets
- Strategic analysis of competitive intelligence
- Investigative methods for global corporations
- Shift from CI tactics to strategies
- Gaining the competitive edge by making use of patent information
- Construction of CI system
- CI protection strategies and countermeasures
- CI in Japan
- Selling of CI and its application to marketing
- The internet and intranet technologies
- Prediction of competitors' future trends
- Competitive markets and CI
- Analysis of competitors' scientific and technological abilities
- Global CI for global competition
- Establishing a Strategic CI Department.

As can be seen from the above, the CIA-style competitive intelligence research remains as the mainstream of the study at SCIP.

2.3. Competitive Intelligence consultants

CI consultancy firms have begun to emerge in Europe. Their areas of expertise include new business development, organizational reconstruction, strategic alliances, acquisition, and expansion. The following are some of their services that utilize CI strategies:

- Collection and analysis of CI (field surveys of market trends and of domestic and international competitors, and assessment of performance and strategies);
- Baseline assessment (to quantify sales, profits, market shares, and technical innovation of major competitors, and to rank and track competitors);
- Benchmarking (to set leading companies and competitors as the benchmark, and then compare clients' performance with theirs, i.e., compare and examine them in categories such as raw materials, workforce, sales, R&D, production costs, product quality, procurement, and advertising, for clients' competitive edge);
- Survey of consumers' opinions and needs;
- Vulnerability assessment of competitors' clients;
- Analyzing and determining the possibility of new projects, new products, and new markets (to determine whether or not to enter a new market, to evaluate competitors' strategies, and to analyze customer needs and the maturity of new fields, profits, growth rate, and alternative products);
- Gathering information related to acquisition, joint venture, and business partners;
- Researching the country's political situation, its regulations, competitors' trends there, and its market, when advancing overseas;
- Researching trends in new technologies, new product development, and emerging markets, and tracking them;
- BI education.

The above are the main areas that CI consultancy firms work in. By providing clients with such BI, they help contribute to clients' decision-making in corporate strategies in obtaining the competitive edge.

3. Human Resources Development for Business Intelligence

3.1. Business Intelligence research and educational institutions

Due to rising CI research among intelligence agencies, business, and academia in Europe and the US, the efficacy of business and competitive intelligence has begun to gain recognition in overseas business schools. In particular, Lund University in Sweden, where Dr. Stevan Dedijer brought the importance of BI research to the attention of the world in 1972, has a course on BI and security protection, and its School of Economics and Management confers master's and doctoral degrees in BI. Below is a summary of the current situation of intelligence education in intelligence research and educational institutes and business schools in the US, France, Sweden and Australia.

a. The United States of America

- Academy of Competitive Intelligence (ACI)

  Ben Gilad (former Associate Professor at Rutgers University), Leonard Fuld (President of Fuld & Company, an American competitive intelligence research company), and Jan Herring (a former CIA operative) founded the ACI in Boston. It offers students and corporate employees various CI programs, and also provides CIA operatives with training. Apart from the ACI, the National Defense University in the US offers military and BI programs, too.

- Rutgers Business School

  Rutgers Business School is an active center of CI education in the US. Its curricula includes the following:

  o Analysis of CI, with emphasis on theory and practice — use of the case method.
  o Management strategy and competitive strategy.
  o Case study — Kodak versus Polaroid, GE versus Westing House.

- o Topics covered: study of competitive trends in pharmaceutical and food industries, American companies' intelligence strategy, competitive analysis, environmental analysis and strategy decision-making, construction of effective intelligence systems for competitive edge, study of decision-making support system, environmental scan of American multinational corporations, study of management thinking, and intelligence needs analysis for top management.
- o Available intelligence and use of intelligence sources. Intelligence gathering methods. Utilization of intelligence systems and networks. Market and customer information. Technical information. Productivity information. Experiments and search. Cultural, political, and social environment information. Research on global CI systems.

b. *France*

- Ecole de Guerre Economique (EGE) — School of Economic Warfare

  Founded by Christitan Harbulot in Paris, 1997. Here, middle management learns global strategies to secure shares in the global market, and studies CI with the idea that 97% of necessary information is publicly available. EGE has a close relationship with the nation's Ministry of Defense.

c. *Sweden*

- Sweden Business Intelligence Center

  Founded in Stockholm in 1997, by business, academia and the military in preparation for the coming Intelligence War. It promotes intelligence research.

- Lund University

  Lund University offers theories and practical knowledge on BI. Its syllabus includes a five-year course on "Business Intelligence and Confidentiality." Some of the areas covered in lectures are comprehensive industry analysis, competition analysis, corporate information systems, and organizational knowledge transfer. Below is part of its typical curriculum:

o Theory: Business intelligence's history and purpose; Strategies, marketing, finances, organizational learning; Organizations' external environment; Intelligence cycle as a model of intelligence activity; Necessity and utilization of intelligence — resources for information search, storing information, analysis and presentation; Legal and ethical problems; Recognition, organization, political information and their limits; Management overview, policies, strategies and their prospects.

o Guest lecturers — Corporate intelligence analysts give lectures on how they utilize BI in practice.

o Case study — Students are required to study solutions for matters relating to intelligence, and to carry out practical research.

d. *Australia*

• Graduate School of Business, the University of Technology, Sydney

The course, "Global Business and Competitive Intelligence," is offered here, in the belief that utilization of competitive intelligence is vital to companies for enhancing their global competitiveness. Companies must continually monitor the rapidly changing business environment, yet the traditional management information system does not allow them to track global opportunities and risks. On the other hand, contemporary information systems can confuse decision-makers by offering too much information. Herein lies the need for intelligence.

3.2. *Urgent need for Business Intelligence programs*

BI and CI have therefore been studied in Western universities and business schools for quite some time now. Cutting-edge information processing techniques, including those of the CIA's, are adopted in information collection, analysis and utilization at graduate schools; the study of practical application is also quite actively pursued.

As global competition grows ever fiercer, global BI programs should be introduced at university levels in Japan, too. Its early introduction is key to developing human resources that would enable the country to survive global competition in the era of the Internet.

Chapter 5

Intelligence and Patent Disputes

The US Senate Committee on Intelligence held a joint hearing on industrial espionage on February 28, 1996. Based on the Committee's proposal, President Clinton signed off on the "Economic Espionage Act of 1996" on October 11. This marked the beginning of the counter-intelligence war.

1. The Background of the Economic Espionage Act

The Economic Espionage Act, which the FBI and business experts in America spent two years drafting, applies to not only foreign economic espionage, but also domestic theft of trade secrets.

The FBI initiated the Economic Counter-intelligence Program towards the end of 1994. Its objective was to investigate and prevent foreign espionage which might threaten America's economic interests. The program's legal measures, however, proved to be ineffective against rapidly increasing economic espionage.

Therefore, as noted in Chapter 2, Section 3, the Economic Espionage Act of 1996 adopted more stringent punitive measures on national security grounds. Not only does it give the FBI the power to indict unlawful espionage, but it also provides for extraterritorial jurisdiction. Article 1831 dictates a punishment of a $500,000 fine or 15-year jail sentence for individuals who act as industrial spies on behalf of foreign countries. For corporations and organizations, they would be charged a fine of $10 million. This is quite a severe punishment, compared to the $4,500 fine that the

Japanese judiciary had once imposed on Dai-Ichi Kangyo Bank for illegal activities.

In order to enhance America's competitiveness at a time when mega-competition in information, telecommunications, high technology and service industry had started, the Clinton administration focused its efforts on expanding export and promoting the information and telecommunications industry. In particular, it deemed that protection of economic intelligence, biotechnology industry and high technology was vital for competing in the global market.

Some argue that the Economic Espionage Act is targeted at European countries — especially France — and Japan. Therefore, those who are engaged in survey, planning, and R&D in the Japanese government, organizations, research institutes, and corporations must exercise due caution. More sensitive handling would be required in dealing with American corporations and in intelligence activities in the US.

One famous case of espionage scandal involving a Japanese corporation is the case of Fujitsu's intelligence activities against Fairchild Semiconductor which lasted for a period of ten years beginning in 1976. It became notorious as Fujitsu was suspected of illegally collecting information from local workers in order to purchase 80% of Fairchild Semiconductor's shares. There have also been other cases like the Honeywell–Minolta patent dispute and the Toshiba Machine Company affair.

It is said that 97% of necessary information can be obtained from the public domain such as newspapers, journals and TV, and also through private means. It is unethical to risk breaking the law and resort to illegal measures and spying to obtain the confidential information, which is a mere 3% of the whole necessary information; not to mention, it is a waste of time, money and effort. Such attempts at securing confidential information by unethical measures — activities that might infringe on the Economic Espionage Act — must be avoided at all costs.

We must estimate competitors' ability, intentions and competitive environment, and determine corporate strategies, based on lawful and ethical collection and analysis of information. In my personal experience, in cases of newly acquired business, 40% of the information necessary for the success I obtained from the public domain, while 60% was from the private domain.

However, according to the Senate Committee on Intelligence, 51 countries are currently engaged in economic espionage in the US, competing in collection of confidential information and taking advantage of the nation's policy of active disclosure. Among those, 23 nations are most active in their espionage activities, the FBI revealed. The White House Office of Science and Technology Policy estimates that damage to the nation by industrial espionage amounts to $100 billion per year. ABC News reports that six million people have lost their jobs over the past decade because of economic espionage. The White House has announced a plan to invest $2 trillion in fund research in ten years. Such research projects, however, are prime targets for foreign governments and corporations, as the intellectual property rights are not securely protected. Innovative high-tech industry is said to be especially damaged by industrial spying.

Economic intelligence is vital for American corporations to maintain their competitive edge. Therefore, the White House has set revitalization of the American economy as one of its crucial policies, believing economic intelligence to be the most important factor in economic security, which has become inseparable from national security since the end of the Cold War.

Previously, it was predicted by 13 major computer companies that the US would sustain damages of between $40 billion to $80 billion due to computer crimes. The American government therefore warned corporations in Silicon Valley and San Jose, which constitute one-third of the American high-tech industry, that they were targeted by foreign industrial spies.

Nevertheless, one of Intel's employees managed to steal a design for Pentium microprocessor, and sold it to Cuba, North Korea, Iraq, China, Iran, the USSR and the Eastern European countries. He later confessed to the FBI that he had been selling technological information concerning cutting-edge micro devices to the Cuban intelligence service for ten years. Senator Baucus, alarmed by the situation, requested to the Senate Committee on Intelligence that both the FBI and the CIA make further efforts to protect economic and high-tech confidential information.

The FBI has revealed that it investigated 800 cases of economic espionage, in which 23 nations were involved. In addition, the American Society for Industrial Security conducted a survey of 325 companies and discovered 700 cases of infringement on intellectual property rights. The total damage amounted to $5.1 billion.

In a separate case related to the biotechnology industry, two pharmaceutical companies invested $750 million in fermentation technology; however, an employee was arrested by an undercover FBI agent when attempting to sell this technology for $1.5 million. Another case involved an attempted theft of Tomahawk cruise missiles' bid statement; an undercover FBI agent arrested an employee who tried to sell it for $50,000. The American Navy had been planning to award the contract to either Hughes Aircraft Company or McDonnell Douglas Corporation for $3 billion.

2. The Start of Economic Intelligence War

It was during the Carter administration that the American intelligence services began showing an interest in economic matters. President Carter appointed Admiral Stansfield Turner as the Director of Central Intelligence in 1977. Admiral Turner's major achievement is said to be being the first DCI to recognize the importance of economic intelligence. He predicted that economic intelligence would become more important than defense information for national defense and security.

Admiral Turner emphasized the importance of counter-intelligence against foreign nations' economic espionage in *Foreign Affairs* in 1991. He eloquently asserted that America should openly participate in an economic intelligence war, thus making him a prophet of the Intelligence War Era.

Pichot-Duclos, the president of a renowned military intelligence school in France — a nation that is at intelligence war with the United States in the aircraft industry — also noted that economic intelligence had become the post-Cold War weapon. Meanwhile, the foreign intelligence service (BND) of Germany — a key nation in the EU — is said to have warned that the US intelligence services were feeding American corporations technological information of foreign corporations, and likewise, started to provide German companies with confidential information that BND obtained overseas. China, which had been moving towards a socialist market economy through the reform and "open door" policies, began its study of business intelligence with the establishment of the Competitive Intelligence Association of China in April 1995. This organization played an important role in the shift in the Chinese economic system.

A further surprise for the US Senate Committee on Intelligence was the news that President Yeltsin gave orders to the Russian high officials on February 7, 1996, to maximize their efforts on collecting information regarding advanced nations' technology, economy and industry, in order to catch up with the West in technology. Senator Arlen Specter of the Senate Committee on Intelligence warned that foreign nations' agents and corporations were now targeting not just American citizens, companies and industries, but the American government itself in their attempts to steal confidential economic information.

Since the Internet has made a mass of information freely available online, we are now in the middle of an Intelligence War, with no distinction between the West and the former Soviet nations, but rather, with all of them scrambling to win. A fierce international competition, whose weapon of choice is information, has begun in the global market, where effective demand expanded from one billion to three billion people after the end of the Cold War.

I have participated as a speaker at SCIP international conferences in America and at intelligence conferences in France. Based on these experiences, I got the impression that the Western information professionals considered the Japan External Trade Organization (JETRO) and other Japanese trading companies to be a center for economic espionage activities, and overestimated their intelligence abilities. Consequently, I believe that the Japanese government and companies should launch more active and effective public relations projects so that the real situation would become known and this ungrounded misunderstanding would be cleared up.

What strategies do American and European companies adopt in the era of Business Intelligence War? As has already been mentioned several times, the Society of Competitive Intelligence Professionals (SCIP) was founded in America in 1986, in order to apply intelligence techniques and competitive intelligence techniques to business. Its members are mainly military intelligence officials, corporate workers in planning and R&D departments, consultants, and intelligence researchers at research institutes and universities.

With the vision of penetrating into EU nations, SCIP has branched out into Europe and has held conferences in Vienna and Brussels, where the EU headquarters is based. Among the topics covered at these conferences were CI strategic analytical techniques, CI processing ability development, knowledge transfer and online information gathering, corporate decision-making, skill development and construction of corporate knowledge base, and corporate innovation and competitive advantage strategies. SCIP also has a branch in France, which is an active center of intelligence research in Europe; representatives of major French corporations and multinational companies gather there frequently to hold conferences.

Over in London, the Association for Global Strategic Information (AGSI) was established in 1992, and it has held annual conferences since then. The Global Business Development Alliance was founded in Geneva in 1996, of which I was a vice chairman. The alliance, whose main founding members were American and French intelligence professionals, and whose main members were multinational companies' executives, conducted research on development of new business on a global scale, by making use of business intelligence and global networks of connections.

As for Asia and Oceania, SCIP Australia conducts research on CI. Also, as mentioned before, the Association of Competitive Intelligence of China was established in 1995. This is an academic organization, based on the Institute of Scientific and Technical Information of China, whereby approximately 20,000 members from over 400 research networks are engaged in theoretical and practical studies of CI.

Compared to such active research among American, European and Asian companies, it cannot be denied that Japan appears to lag behind. The Business Intelligence Society of Japan, which I established in 1992, has held seminars on business intelligence, in contact with the American SCIP and French and Chinese intelligence professionals, every other month for the last 17 years. It is my fear, however, that unless the government and industry tackle the issue of intelligence strategies seriously, Japan will fall behind other Asian countries, not just Europe and America, in the increasingly fierce global intelligence competition.

3. Major Cases of Intelligence/Patent Disputes between Japan and America

3.1. *The Fujitsu–Fairchild Semiconductor merger deal*

At the time of the merger, Fairchild Semiconductor was a wholly-owned subsidiary of a French company, Schlumberger, but the US Department of Defense and Department of Commerce nevertheless objected to the transaction on the grounds of high-technology protection. Objections were raised to protect America's national interests. The problem here was that no legal grounds existed to oppose the acquisition. Since then, the Exon-Florio Provision has been implemented to block foreign acquisition of American companies if national security or industrial policies are infringed.

3.2. *The Honeywell–Minolta patent dispute*

On February 7, 1992, the US District Court in New York ruled that Minolta had infringed on Honeywell's patent on AF technology, and ordered Minolta to pay $96,350,000. Minolta's mid-term closing had ended with a deficit of 2.1 billion yen, and it therefore had to downsize and sell off its assets in order to meet this payment. Although Honeywell had already pulled out from the camera industry, patenting remained its basic corporate strategy, and it went on to sue 15 other companies for patent infringement.

Minolta was banned from conducting further sales in the US, and the final settlement was $127,500,000. The company's total loss amounted to 25 billion yen, on top of the massive legal fee of two billion yen. Inspired by this success, Honeywell subsequently sued other Japanese companies such as Canon, Nikon, Olympus, and Asahi Kogaku for patent infringement. All the companies except Canon settled, while Nikon paid $45 million to Honeywell.

It can be concluded from this that America's jury system may not work to Japan's advantage. Therefore, Japanese companies should take such measures as hiring capable attorneys, signing cross-licensing agreements, and strengthening their legal departments.

3.3. *The Toshiba COCOM affair — exporting machine tools to the Soviet Union*

This incident is said to have come to light through a leak from an ex-branch manager of Toshiba Machine Company's rival company. The US Department of Defense subsequently filed a complaint on military grounds and insisted that America had incurred losses of $30 billion from this deal, and demanded damages of $8 billion. The Tokyo District Court sentenced Toshiba Machine's two employees who were in charge of this transaction to ten months and one year in prison, respectively, with a stay of execution for three years, for breaching COCOM agreements. Meanwhile, America placed a three-year embargo on Toshiba products. Toshiba's losses were estimated to be 15 billion yen. Japan's Ministry of Foreign Affairs and Ministry of International Trade and Industry reportedly indicted Toshiba, instead of protecting it, and Toshiba was forced to publish apologies in American newspapers and magazines.

What was problematic with this case was that although Toshiba Machine's machine tools were exported to the USSR in 1982, the Soviet submarines' screw noises had already been lessened since 1979. However, a thorough investigation was not conducted in fear of offending the US. Japanese ministries' weak-kneed response was one contributing factor to this case. The economic friction between America and Japan is considered to be a remote cause.

I believe that America's military strategy of export control against the Communist camp, its economic strategies, and its policies to protect national interests must have been behind this case. America attacked the Japanese government and companies by extraterritorial application of its domestic laws.

3.4. *Other lawsuits between Japan and America*

(a) 1987 — Genentech vs. Toyobo: patent dispute over thrombolytics
(b) 1990 — Sega Enterprises lost a case to an American private inventor
(c) 1992 — Loral Fairchild vs. Sony: CCD patent infringement
(d) 1993 — IBM vs. Kyocera: a lawsuit over unauthorized copying of PC
(e) 1995 — Cray vs. NEC: computer technology dispute
(f) 1996 — NEC anti-dumping case: NEC chose to go to court
(g) 1996 — the US Department of Justice vs. Ajinomoto and Kyowa Hakko: international cartel dispute over fodder additives (both companies were fined one billion yen for Anti-Monopoly Law violations)

The above is evidence of America's war in high technology, biotechnology, and Alzheimer research. There seem to lie behind it America's strategies to deliberately attack Japan for the sake of its own national interests, so that America could secure hegemony in biotechnology, along with information and telecommunications technologies.

What is notable here is that the Economic Espionage Act was applied only about 20 times in the first five years after it was enacted in 1996. It seems deliberate that the first indictment under the EEA involving foreign agents was the aforementioned 2001 case of a Japanese chemist at the Cleveland Clinic Institute who was charged with theft of the Alzheimer's disease research materials. This case should have been defended more vigorously. Thus, there is an urgent need for Japan to enact its own Economic Espionage Act.

4. Risks that Japanese Corporations are Facing

4.1. *How I came to study risk management*

I had lived overseas in seven different countries for 20 years and visited over 60 countries while working for a trading company for 33 years. During that time, I experienced some failures due to badly managed information gathering and negligence, and also saw other companies incur great losses due to failure in risk management. This made me realize that in global business management, not making a loss comes before making money, and that risk management is more important than anything else for this purpose.

During my stay in Iraq from 1966 to 1969, we faced a claim regarding the quality of products in our fabric business, which led me to recognize the importance of quality control in strict accordance with agreements. It is also important to thoroughly collect information about buyers' personalities and business customs. We cannot be cautious enough in business, as once a claim is raised, it takes a lot of time until it is resolved.

When I was in India from 1970 to 1974, we had problems in the tyre and wool business because of fluctuations in the dollar and yen exchange rates; either the exporting company or the importing one had to bear the losses caused by the exchange rate fluctuations. In hindsight, both companies should have entered into a forward contract. In the end, the matter was solved by both companies sharing the loss. The moral of this tale is that gathering information about trends in world economy and exchange rates is vital for global business (see Figure 3).

In addition, during my stay in Brazil from 1974 to 1979, I witnessed my company's misfortune; my colleague's transmission line tower project fell through due to poor marketing as well as the Brazilian government's repression, and we had to sell our factory and pull out of the country. We had not conducted sufficient research and planning before moving operations to Brazil. This represented a failure in risk management.

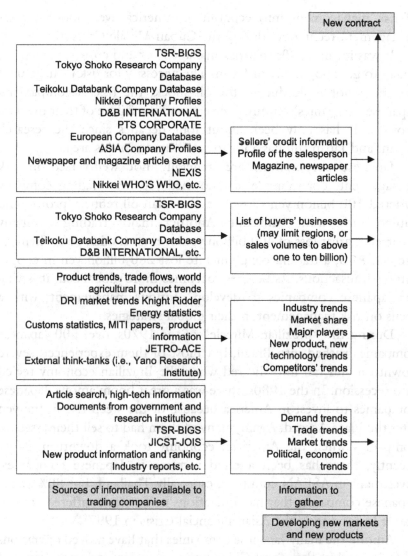

Figure 3: Information Sources for Trading Companies

Source: N-Trading Company's data.

4.2. *Japanese companies' risk management*

Risk management originated in 1920s Germany under conditions of heavy inflation, as a theory of management policy to provide companies with management know-how for corporate protection. Subsequently, the French economist Henri Fayol introduced the idea of risk management into economics. America even adopted crisis management techniques during the Cuban Missile Crisis in 1962.

It was in the 1970s that risk management and crisis management began to gain popularity in Japan. The necessity for risk management became a hot topic due to the oil shock, the risks accompanying Japanese companies' venture overseas, and the failure of their overseas projects. It has only been about four decades since the research began, and Japan still has a lot to catch up on in this area.

Japanese corporations are generally not well-versed in risk management. For example, a renowned Japanese trading company suffered 100 billion yen's loss in a Canadian oil refinery project and subsequently went bankrupt. Another major trading company incurred a great loss of 400 billion yen over an Iranian petrochemical project. Also, a trading conglomerate lost 280 billion yen in copper futures transactions. As business becomes more globalized, it is vital for Japanese companies to develop cautious management, with a focus on risk management in their global strategies.

During the "Brazilian Miracle" of the 1970s, over 500 Japanese companies rushed into Brazil, but most of them experienced severe downturn and ran into the red when the Brazilian economy reeled into recession. In the 1980s, there was a great boom among Japanese companies to invest in America because of the steep rise in the yen after the Plaza Accord. Again, many of them had to sell their assets or companies when the American economy took a downturn. More recently, there has been a rapid increase in Japanese companies' investment in ASEAN countries, especially Thailand, but 80% of the Japanese companies that had operations in Thailand suffered considerable losses during the Asian Financial Crisis in 1997.

Among the many Japanese companies that have moved operations to China amidst the recent China boom, some are losing money, and some have moved their production base to other South Eastern nations such as India, due to demonstrations and other unstable political elements.

Japanese companies do not seem to be aware of the gravity of these risks. Some seem to embark on overseas operations without any concrete management strategy, but merely following other companies' lead. Careless expansion without proper prior research could turn into a nightmare. What is necessary in global business is multilateral, comprehensive risk and crisis management; not simply risk management, but risk, crisis, and emergency risk management.

4.3. *Global risks that Japanese companies face*

After the fall of the Berlin Wall brought about the end of the Cold War, the former USSR Eastern European countries shifted towards a market economy, and China adopted reform and "open door" policies, moving rapidly towards a socialist-oriented market economy. Vietnam promoted the *doi moi* policy, India opened its market to the world economy, and a new gigantic market of Brazil, Russia, India and China (BRICs) emerged. Free trade areas are spreading as more countries enter FTAs. Furthermore, the emerging threat of terrorism, the subprime mortgage crisis that originated in America, and other rapid changes in the world economy and politics have embroiled Japan in rocketing global risks, as globalization of business increasingly puts Japan in closer relationships with these countries through commerce, investment, corporate alliances, technical cooperation, and expansion of business overseas. Under these circumstances, management of financial crisis, country risk, emergency risk, and other crises have become vital for global management strategies.

As Japanese companies become more globalized, with more corporations venturing overseas, business risk has risen exponentially. We must take special note of political and economic risks such as country risk, terrorism, political unrest, the growing gap of wealth between developed and developing countries, investment risk, foreign exchange risk, and financial risk; and also the safety and security of employees sent to overseas operations, and their danger and emergency management. In addition, although business with BRICs is expected to grow, business risk in the emerging market is already on the rise.

It is imperative that we collect information through legal means and make use of it, so that we can manage ever-increasing risk by accurate analysis. We must search for ways to predict risks and crises in advance and then try to prevent them (see Table 1).

Table 1: Cases Where Use of Intelligence Led to Success

No.	Source	Information	Business	Amount	Note
1	Industrial magazine (public information)	Shortage of raw materials for chemical fibers	Sales of raw materials for chemical fibers	10 million dollars	Contract
2	Local tyre battery agent	Middle East will boycott American and European import cars after the Six-Day War	First case of exporting 2,000 Japanese cars	500 million yen	Re-contract
3	Local Asian newspaper	Shortage of raw materials for pharmaceutical products	First case of exporting penicillin and streptomycin	500 million yen	Re-contract
4	Tokyo	Asian Development Bank will tender a bid for irrigation machines	First case of exporting bulldozers to Southwest Asia	500 million yen	The deal took 4 years to finalize
5	An engineer	There will be an open tender for microwaves in Central and South America	Export of microwaves, EAXs, and optical fiber	500 million yen	Re-contract
6	Local agent	South America will lift the embargo on cars	Exporting 40,000 cars	50 billion yen	The deal took 2 years. Re-contract
7	Local collaborator	Grant aid projects	First case of exporting medical equipments and TV facilities (Central and South America)	500 million yen	Led to a similar business with Central and South America

(*Continued*)

Table 1:   (*Continued*)

No.	Source	Information	Business	Amount	Note
8	Local collaborator	South America grant aid projects	First case of selling agricultural equipments	100 million yen	The deal took 1 year to finalize
9	Tokyo	Gas pipeline plan in Asia	Collaborated with a North American pipeline construction and management company (their know-how; Japanese pipes and finances)	10 billion yen	Re-contract
10	Tokyo	An open tender for casing pipes in the Communist camp	Sold pipes to a North American engineering company	1 billion yen	The deal took 1 year to finalize
11	Information magazine by embassy's commercial department	Possibility of importing graphics information systems	Technical alliance with a North American company	50 million yen	The deal took 1 year to finalize
12	A local newspaper in North America	An innovative medical imaging system was invented	Exclusive distributorship	50 million yen	The deal took 3 years to finalize
13	A customer in North America	A company is looking to buy printing machines	First case of selling coating machines to North America	1.3 billion yen	The deal took 2 years to finalize

(*Continued*)

Table 1:   (*Continued*)

No.	Source	Information	Business	Amount	Note
14	Trade show in North America	Hi-Tec acquired new technology, new business information	Introduced telemarketing and catalogue business targeted at Japan	—	Failed
15	North American trade magazine article	Hi-Tec looking to sell in Japan	Tried to sell electronic filing systems and machine translators	—	Failed

Source: "Role of intelligence for trading companies," "JAFT," 30 March 1993, p. 114.

4.4. *Strengthening Japanese companies' risk management policies*

The best tool for risk management is gathering accurate information. We must practice accurate analysis and assessment of information, and making decisions based on that intelligence, on a regular basis. It is possible to predict risks and crises beforehand and prevent them by analysis and management of risks.

As Japanese companies become globalized, various potential crises arise, and these are of greater magnitude than before, as recent financial crises show. Japanese companies' top management must become well-versed in risk and crises management, and establish secure risk and crisis management systems. They must also be equally alert to protection of confidential information and of technical and intellectual property.

For effective risk management, we need to build a system which enables us to respond to risks quickly, and we must enhance our ability to gather, evaluate, analyze, utilize and predict risk information. That is to say, we must manage risks strategically and eliminate them before they cause any harm. From symptomatic therapy to risk prevention — that is the key to managing growing risks in this business environment of global, growing competition.

Chapter 6

The Current Situation of Intelligence Education in America and France

1. International Intelligence Education

1.1. *Privatization of intelligence*

When intelligence officials of American and European intelligence agencies began taking up teaching positions in departments of intelligence, research, planning and sales in the private sector, the intelligence guru, Stevan Dedijer of Lund University, Sweden, referred to it as "Privatization of Intelligence." He predicted that governments and business would increasingly collaborate in intelligence activities.

In fact, the strengthening of intelligence education and collaboration in intelligence activities amongst the military, the government, industry and academia are rapidly progressing in the US out of regret that 9/11 was not predicted and prevented. I had a strong impression that this was so, when I participated in the annual conference of the International Association for Intelligence Education (IAFIE) held in the suburbs of Washington, D.C. In keeping with this trend, the Japanese government should make intelligence education a top priority, too.

In the meantime, Ecole Européenne d'Intelligence Economique (EEIE) was opened in Versailles in September 2006. France is one of the most active centers of intelligence education in Europe, and is quick to respond to the intelligence education trends in America. More details on this will follow later in Section 3 of this chapter.

1.2. *International conferences for intelligence education*

Approximately 120 intelligence professionals from the military, governments, business and academia, mainly from the US and Canada, participated in the IAFIE's conference mentioned above. Patrick Kennedy, Deputy Director of National Intelligence; Michael McConnell, former Director of the National Security Agency; Graham B. Spanier, President of the Pennsylvania State University; and Professor Christopher Andrew from University of Cambridge all delivered keynote speeches.

The conference was mainly focused on national security, counter-terrorism measures, and education for those purposes. In light of 9/11, there was a great emphasis on the necessity for the entire nation — the military, governments, industry and academia alike — to collaborate in the efforts for comprehensive intelligence education. Especially heated was the discussion about what kind of intelligence education should be carried out at university and graduate school levels.

Intelligence had already been privatized in America when the Society of Competitive Intelligence Professionals (SCIP) was founded in Virginia by intelligence professionals encompassing various fields. Approximately 1,200 intelligence professionals from various parts of the world participated in the SCIP's 20th annual international conference, held in Orlando, Florida in April 2006. However, there were only five Japanese participants including myself at the conference, which showed Japan's lack of interest in intelligence, and how behind we are in these matters.

1.3. *Rising international intelligence education*

As I have mentioned several times already, the Academy of Competitive Intelligence (ACI) was founded by intelligence professionals and academics in Boston, and has been actively providing intelligence education since, mainly to corporate employees. It offers certified courses during the spring and fall seasons, in which competitive information gathering, analysis, and utilization techniques of the military and intelligence agencies are taught. It has started to provide intelligence education in Europe too in recent years, with a campus located in Belgium. Alumni of this academy who work in research, planning, and strategic management departments of corporations are devoted to information gathering, analysis, and utilization, conducting research on global competitors, in their attempts to gain competitive advantage in the ever-more fiercely competitive global market.

On the other hand, the International Association for Intelligence Education (IAFIE) is relatively new; it was established in June 2004. Yet its membership encompasses American intelligence professionals in all fields — individual members, students, corporate members, sponsoring companies, universities, the military and government officials. Its executive director is a former Director of the Central Intelligence Agency. The association plans to expand into Asia in the future, and has requested Japan's help in organizing international conferences in Asia.

At the IAFIE's annual conference mentioned above, many voiced their opinion that the curriculum for nationwide systematic and effective intelligence education and standard textbooks, and application of intelligence education techniques to business — not just to the military, administration and academic study — should be reviewed, in order to fortify global competitiveness. The importance of language studies, especially of Arabic, Chinese and Russian, along with cultural studies, was also pointed out. Participants came from Brazil and the Czech Republic, as well as the US, the UK and Canada. Only two Japanese, including myself, were there.

1.4. *Closer cooperation of the public and private sectors in intelligence education*

The IAFIE's principal objectives are national security, enforcement of the law, and closer cooperation of the public and private sectors as a catalyst among competitive intelligence professionals. The association places an emphasis on educating the nation's next generation — university and graduate school students — on information gathering, analysis, and utilization, and also on spreading public order, security, and counter-terrorism measures to the world, not just within the US.

For that purpose, it advocates closer collaboration of the military, governments, business and academia in intelligence education, and it also promotes studies and training of intelligence theories, intelligence education, and intelligence usage methods, with the aim of developing and sharing knowledge and expertise.

Given the current issue of Iran's nuclear weapons, the Arab Spring uprisings, and recent new appointments within the CIA, it is expected that America will become more active in its intelligence activities, including competitiveness building. Under such circumstances, Japan must immediately establish its own national intelligence agency too, to conduct intelligence activities that include business intelligence, and to strengthen intelligence education.

2. Curricula of Intelligence Education in America

2.1. *The Academy of Competitive Intelligence*

- Competitive Intelligence Professional Certificate Program
- Fee per day: US$1,150–US$1,350

a. *Intelligence sources & collection techniques (Fuld/Sandman)*

- Create intelligence and identify state-of-the-art sources.
- Apply the most efficient and effective strategies for finding and analyzing information.
- Analyze privately-held companies and subsidiaries.
- Use the latest Internet intelligence tools and techniques.
- Confirm rumors and improve management decision-making.
- Develop rapid-fire team intelligence-gathering strategies.
- Practice intelligence-gathering from human sources.
- Textbook: *The Secret Language of Competitive Intelligence* by Leonard Fuld (Random House, 2006).

b. *Competitive benchmarking & tactical analysis (Fuld/Sandman)*

- Benchmark actual business practices and costs of competitors.
- Anticipate a company's near-term tactical moves.
- Construct an early warning approach to monitor a rival's changing product, service and market shifts.
- Cut through a competitor's smokescreen to accurately anticipate and prepare for a competitor's new product roll-out.
- Learn the triggers that motivate management to use intelligence expediently.
- Special lecture: Account Analysis — intelligence-gathering from figures.

c. *Competitive blindspots (Gilad)*

- Predict your industry's evolution paths.
- Understand competitors' behaviors and predict significant competitive moves.
- Pinpoint competitors' soft spots, blindspots, and strategic vulnerabilities.
- Assess the importance of information and the right questions to ask your collection network.
- Evaluate your own company's strategy and its blindspots, as well as pinpoint its vulnerabilities.
- Identify sources of critical change in the market.
- Create proactive intelligence to preempt competitors' strategic moves.
- Textbook: *Early Warning* by Ben Gilad (Amacom, 2003).

d. *Cross-competitor analysis (Gilad)*

- Refine your understanding of competitors' behavior when there are several significant competitors.
- Use strategic mapping — a tool no intelligence analyst should do without and no executive should overlook.

- Analyze paradigm shifts in industries undergoing rapid change or transition.
- Test your ability to make predictions about industries and competitors based on assumptions and minimal data.
- Discover nuances and complexities of analyzing divisions and subsidiaries of holding companies and large diversified parent companies.
- Use analytical frameworks, such as demand analysis, lifecycle analysis, and portfolio analysis in evaluating competitors, customers and partners.

e. *Creating and running a world-class intelligence operation (Herring/Gilad)*

- Establish the professional intelligence process used by successful CI organizations worldwide.
- Choose the right CI structure for your company or business unit.
- Choose the right personnel for managing and leading intelligence-oriented strategies.
- Create a user-needs identification process and develop measure-of-effectiveness (MOE) and value (ROI) assessment systems.
- Use all three basic intelligence operations to produce actionable intelligence.
- Intelligence products and how to make use of them.

f. *Anticipating innovation (Paap)*

- Identify the fundamentals of innovation, i.e., the intelligence component in developing successful breakthrough products and services.
- Uncover hidden drivers to anticipate emerging or unarticulated needs.
- Anticipate new and potentially disruptive technologies — key elements of technology forecasting.
- Use Technology Scouting to adapt solutions from other industries.
- Position the development and launch through competitor analysis.
- Avoid being blindsided by the innovative efforts of others.

g. *War gaming: theory & practice (Gilad)*

- Strategic selection and evaluation.
- Respond immediately to new trends in the market.
- Build scenarios for future industries.
- Brainstorming for creative competitive act.
- Create war games for effective results.

h. *Value chain analysis (Gilad)*

- Understand the real strategic differences in value chain activities between your company and its competitors.
- Identify major cost drivers for competitors' advantage.
- Understand the various sources of sustainable and non-sustainable competitive advantages.
- Replace SWOT with a significantly more sophisticated framework.
- Use a numerical analysis to identify threats to your company's position.
- Assess which benchmarking has a chance of succeeding and which is just a waste of money.

i. *Scenario analysis (Sandman/Rose)*

- Use the results of Scenario Analysis to craft resilient competitive strategy, despite being faced with highly uncertain competitive conditions.
- Learn methods for developing different "futures" for your company, thereby offering your management potent strategic options.
- Build scenarios, based on first-hand case studies drawn from actual Fuld & Company client engagements.
- Use the results of Scenario Analysis to determine competitive strategy.
- Apply Scenario Analysis as a fundamental building block for your early warning system.

Source: Fuld, Gilad, Herring, "Academy of Competitive Intelligence", Spring 2006.

2.2. i2 Extension University — training future analysts and researchers

Ritchie Martinez, managing director of International Association for Legal Information Analysts, says that law enforcement and the intelligence community keenly feel the shortage of candidates willing to challenge experienced analysts and researchers.

To help fill this void, i2 Extension University offers degrees relating to intelligence and law enforcement, software and support for a master's degree, and it provides colleges and universities with instructor training programs. Based in Mclean, Virginia, i2 is a world-class provider of visual, investigative, and analysis software to the judiciary, the intelligence community, the military and Fortune 500 companies. Over 2,000 organizations in 100 nations rely on i2 for research and intelligence analysis. Its comprehensive intelligence products, which include the award-winning Analyst Notebook, place a special emphasis on quick reporting of analysis results of complex scenarios and seemingly unrelated massive data.

a. *Overview*

- Founded in April 2003.
- Offers seven certification-granting courses: Crime punishment; Public safety; Accounting and economic crimes; Intelligence; National security; Agricultural security; and IT network security. About 6,000 students attend these courses annually.
- Partner universities as of April 2006:

(1) Auburn University
(2) British Columbia Institute of Technology
(3) Central Michigan University
(4) Central Pennsylvania College
(5) Embry-Riddle Aeronautical University
(6) George Mason University
(7) George Washington University
(8) Herkimer County Community College
(9) Herzing University, Birmingham

(10) Hilbert College
(11) Juniata College
(12) Lebanon Valley College
(13) Marshall College
(14) Mercyhurst College
(15) Michigan State University
(16) National Defense University
(17) Naval Postgraduate School
(18) Neumann University
(19) Northeast Wisconsin Technical College
(20) North GA College & State University
(21) University of Notre Dame
(22) Patrick Henry College
(23) Radford University
(24) St. John Fisher College
(25) St. Joseph's College
(26) St. Peter's College
(27) Johns Hopkins University
(28) United States Naval Academy
(29) University of Alabama, Birmingham
(30) University of Central Florida
(31) University of Maine, Augusta
(32) University of Missouri, Columbia
(33) University of New Haven
(34) University of New Mexico
(35) University of Pittsburgh
(36) University of Southern Mississippi
(37) University of Texas, San Antonio
(38) Utica College
(39) West Virginia University
(40) Western Illinois University

2.3. *Liberal studies at Neumann University*

- A 24-unit undergraduate course that provides a theoretical and practical framework for information analysis and various basic studies.

- Covers basic concepts and analytical techniques relating to national security, homeland security, and enforcement.
- A unique program that promotes justice and peace in the spirit of St. Francis of Assisi.
- Basic core programs include major programs in English, liberal arts and political science.
- Specialized intelligence research course includes cutting-edge electronic information study.
- Serves as a preparatory course for acquiring comprehensive knowledge necessary for interdisciplinary cultural study, including language studies that are necessary for national security analysis, especially those vitally important foreign languages.

2.4. *Intelligence analyst course at University of Notre Dame*

Courses:

(a) *Introduction to Intelligence*

In this course, students will study the history and development of intelligence and intelligence officials in the United States of America. Emphasis is on policymakers as clients for information processing, information analysis and intelligence; the issue of restructuring the US intelligence community; supervisory responsibility and accountability; and counter-intelligence and espionage. Students will also discuss the ethical issues of intelligence activities.

(b) *Investigation and Analysis*

This course will aim to develop students' skills and ability necessary for basic intelligence analysis. Relevant skills include planning and coordinating information-gathering from various sources, utilizing analytical techniques during investigation, and transmitting knowledge through intelligence activities. Workshops are focused on detailed discussion, utilizing public information, investigation reports and oral reports.

(c) *Terrorism*

Terrorism as a form of political violence has become a major concern of the world today and is a serious threat to national security. Therefore, in this course, students will study the nature and range of international terrorism, focusing on the mechanisms that the federal government and national security agencies employ to predict and prevent terrorism. The role of intelligence in law enforcement and national security counter-terrorism policies will be discussed in case studies, in which agendas, tactics and funds of actual terrorist groups are analyzed.

(d) *Business Intelligence*

Market research has been practised in business for many years as a tool for management strategy decisions. As companies strive to survive in the fierce competition of today's global market, business intelligence, or competitive intelligence (CI), has become a vital issue for corporate decision-makers. This course will provide a solid foundation for competitive intelligence for studies of information gathering and analysis. Also discussed are ethical matters relating to information gathering, the 1996 Economic Espionage Act, intelligence management and reporting, and building an internal CI function.

(e) *Individual Study Project*

   i. Terrorism
  ii. Information system
 iii. Psychological aspect of foreign culture

Intelligence analysis and research program courses:

- Introduction to the US intelligence

    Overview of doctrines, principles, history and range of intelligence activities, with emphasis on the US intelligence community. Special note on the role of intelligence in democratic society.

- Investigation and analysis methods

  Comprehensive lecture and seminar course to develop basic techniques for intelligence analysis and presentation, and for technical reports.

- Intelligence report writing

  Introduction to effective intelligence reports and presentations. Focuses on intelligence reports, briefing styles, assessment of intelligence products, form and content, and application of various advanced analytical techniques.

- Terrorism

  Its roots and development, and the world today; especially, the origin of terrorism and review of its development, for a clear understanding of terrorism's impact on America.

- Competitive Intelligence

  The study of competitive intelligence and business analysis, and modern business intelligence, with a focus on practical training and public information sources.

- Financial investigation methods

  Background of finance and the techniques that are used in accounting for validating financial frauds, which includes auditing and investigation of various records at analysis centers. This course will cover white-collar crimes, and will emphasize financial crimes, and technical aspects of account data analysis and investigation.

- Intelligence and national security

  Introduction to the US national security decision-making, with special emphasis on the role of intelligence in policy decisions. Covers historical overview and practice of national security after World War II. Lists the major agencies of national security decision-making and its process. Explores major issues of national security and examination of national security in the 21st century.

- Advanced investigation and analysis

  Introduction to further enhancing skills, research and analysis abilities.

- Strategic Intelligence

  This course is divided into three parallel tracks of strategy theory, strategic intelligence practice, and principle application to real life. Students participate in this course as members of an evaluation project group. They will need to submit at least two assessment essays and give a presentation besides various other assignments.

Textbooks:

(1) *The New Competitor Intelligence: The Complete Resource for Finding, Analyzing and Using Information About Your Competitors* by Leonard M. Fuld (John Wiley & Sons, Inc., 1995).

(2) *Confidential: Uncover Your Competitors' Top Business Secrets Legally and Quickly — Protect Your Own* by John Nolan (Yardley-Chambers, 1999).

Main careers of graduates:

- FBI, CIA, Drug Enforcement Administration, the US Secret Service, Defense Intelligence Agency, National Security Agency;
- multinational corporations;
- the federal and state judiciary.

2.5. *Mercyhurst College, Department of Intelligence Studies*

Founded in 1992. It has 220 alumni, and the placement rate for 2005 graduates was 98%. The Center for Information Research, Analysis and Training was founded in 1995. It is well-known nationwide as a pioneer in intelligence education.

a. *Undergraduate program — main courses*

- Introduction to Intelligence Research and Analysis
- Advanced Intelligence Research and Analysis
- Business Intelligence
- Introduction to Criminal Justice Intelligence
- Seminar on Terrorism
- History of US Intelligence and National Security
- Strategic Intelligence
- Intelligence Communications
- Internship/Co-Op

b. *Related courses*

- History (two courses)
- European History Since the Renaissance
- Overview of Anthropology
- American Criminal Justice
- US Government
- Geopolitics
- Macroeconomics
- Statistics
- Foreign Languages (four courses)

c. *Master of Science in Applied Intelligence degree program*

- Theory and Process in Law Enforcement Intelligence
- Intelligence Theories and Applications
- Intelligence Communications
- Topics in Intelligence
- Analyzing Financial Crimes
- Analyzing and Managing Strategic Intelligence
- Thesis in Applied Intelligence

d. *Electives (four courses, 12 units)*

- Leadership & Organizational Behavior
- Graduate Seminar: National Security
- Strategic Business Intelligence

- Studies in Terrorism
- Comparative History of Intelligence
- Advanced Analytical Techniques
- Law Enforcement Intelligence
- Internship/Co-Op

e. *Main members of faculty and staff*

- James G. Breckenridge, M.B.A., M.A., department chair; former faculty member of the History department at West Point; teaches modern European history and Middle East history.
- Robert J. Heibel, M.A., executive director; a retired FBI agent; teaches intelligence, terrorism, Latin American history.
- David J. Grabelski, M.A., assistant professor; former instructor with the US Department of Justice/National Drug Intelligence Center, former Homicide Detective and Gang Unit Supervisor in the Los Angeles Police Department.
- Arthur Mills II, M.A., assistant professor of intelligence studies; former US Department of State Foreign Service Officer; teaches history of intelligence, history of foreign affairs, issues of national security.
- Daniel F. Mulligan, M.A., instructor; manufacturing, sales and consulting, former instructor at West Point; teaches business intelligence.
- Kristan J. Wheaton, M.A., J.D., assistant professor; a retired Foreign Area Officer of the US Army who specializes in national security matters.
- Dawn Wozneak, M.S.; former intelligence analyst for the Federal Bureau of Investigation, former police officer, crime intelligence agency specialist.

2.6. *2006 SCIP International Conference, Orlando, Florida*

a. *Day one (April 27)*

- CI leaders' visions: representatives of Eastman Kodak, Energizer/ Schick-Wilkinson Sword, Wels Fargo, Daimler Chrysler, Business

Intelligence, and Covance discussed recent CI topics, such as how CI is applied in different ways, and how CI meets new demands. Chair: Paul Dishman, Marriott School professor at Brigham Young University.

- Ms. Joan Basset, Senior Vice President of JP Morgan Chase, made a luncheon speech on the strategic development of the intelligence career.
- Development of CI Communication Techniques
- CI for Benefit and Profit in the Federal Market
- Creating & Maintaining Two-Way Communications with Your CI Users
- Mapping Enterprise Risks with Porter's Five Forces to Develop a CI Early Warning System
- State-of-the-Art Tools for More Efficient Info Discovery and Analysis
- Marketing: Building a Visualizing System for CI Team
- Brand Asset Protection: Consumer Journalism Control
- Utilizing Third Parties: How to Partially or Totally Outsource CI Function to External Professionals
- Behind Closed Doors: Getting Information on Companies in Countries with Limited Disclosure Laws
- Breaking New Ground with CI
- Knowledge is Power: Utilizing CI to Improve Strategic Planning
- Sales Ready Scoring: A Novel Use of CI
- What Does Your CEO Really Care About?
- Panel Discussion
- Anticipating Breakthrough Technologies: Using CTI to Leverage Technical Innovations
- CI, Law, and Ethics
- Getting Intelligence Right: It takes a complex adaptive system to cope with a complex adaptive system
- Getting the Most from Your Public Information Source Research
- Threat Awareness: What's CI Got to Do with It?
- Differences are Everywhere: Global CI Practice
- Needed It Yesterday — Expectation of Management
- Threat: What We Need Now

- Analyze This! Assessing Corporate Vulnerabilities
- Export-wise Intelligence
- Lateral Thinking: Improve Your Creative Analysis
- Running the CI Function: Best Practices and Case Studies
- Turning Information Overload into Intelligence Advantage
- Code of Conduct
- Reconstructing the Value Chain: Optimize Organizational Cost Components
- Changes in Environment: Success and Prosperity
- Beyond CI: Best Practices in Competitive Response
- Building a Global CI Community of Practice
- Current Trends in Economic Espionage
- New Software for Decisions and Analysis
- Text and Data Mining — Together at Last

b. *Day two (April 28)*

- "Innovation Management and Obstacles to Innovation: What is to Emerge in Future", special lecture by Harvard Business Professor, Clayton Christensen
- Analyzing the Blogosphere
- Beyond the Obvious: The Role of CI in Strategy
- Ostriches and Eagles: Why Some Companies Soar Up by Using CI While Others Cannot Even Get Hold of CI?
- Panel Presentation: Teaching Competitive Intelligence
- Securing the BrandSpace: The Role of Intelligence in Fighting Brand Piracy
- Panel Presentation: How to Teach CI Analytical Techniques
- AAA: How a Big Brand Stays Relevant through Competitive Intelligence
- Applying Perceptual Mapping for Successful Competitive Positioning
- On-the-Job CI: A Proactive Approach to Career Development
- Tailoring Scenario Planning for Shorter-Term Issues and Challenges
- Discussion Panel

- An Inside Look at How to Optimize a Combined Market Research & Competitive Intelligence Team
- Innovative Telephone Interview by Making the Most Use of CI
- Offensive and Defensive Use of Patents for Competitive Intelligence
- The CI Process and Technology
- Marketing: Visualizing Practice for CI Team
- Assessing the Industry Threats of China's Technological Emergence
- Bird Dogging, Jet Fighter Pilots and Thinking Chameleons — Metaphors and Analogies in CI
- Invisible Competition: Think Differently
- Panel Presentation: Research in Intelligence
- Sea Eye: Christopher Columbus & the Intelligence Process
- Competitive Leveraging of Global Free Trade Agreements
- Finding and Managing the Right CI Provider
- Panel Presentation: Future Directions in Intelligence
- You've Got Data. Now What Do You Do?

c. *Workshop topics 1*

- The Art of the War Game
- What is Intelligence: How to obtain intelligence from simple materials, systematic information gathering, analysis, and value-adding; construction and management of intelligence function
- CIFRAP (Competitive Intelligence Financial Ratio Analytical Process) for Better Executive Decisions
- Doing It the Right Way: The KIT User-Needs Identification Process
- Extreme Presentation — Powerful Communication of Complex and Controversial Intelligence
- From Intelligence to Action; Win Clients' Trust, and Influence Them
- One if by Land: Early Warning in Maturing Industries
- You Know the Question — Where Do You Find the Answer?
- Getting the Most from a Not-So-Secret Weapon: The Internet
- Now, Take the Long View: Applying Future Studies to Your CI Practice

d. *Workshop topics 2*

- Competitive Intelligence Strategy
- Competitor Profiling — Why? How? When?
- Mining and Interpreting Competitive Patent Intelligence
- Practical Tools for Early Warning

e. *Exhibitors*

(1) Academy of Intelligence
(2) Acuity Software
(3) Allis Information Management
(4) Aurora WWDC
(5) Bennion-Robertson, Inc.
(6) Business Intelligence Services, a Thomson Business
(7) C3i Consultants India Pty Ltd. (India)
(8) Cipher Systems, LLC
(9) Competitive Intelligence Services
(10) Current Analysis
(11) Fletcher/CSI
(12) Fuld & Company
(13) Global Intelligence Alliance (Helsinki, Finland)
(14) Moreover, a Verisign Company
(15) Proactive Worldwide, Inc.
(16) Provizio
(17) QL2 Software
(18) SIS International Research
(19) Strategic Analysis, Inc./SAI Information
(20) The Business Intelligence Source
(21) Thomson Scientific
(22) Traction Software
(23) Viva Intelligence Plaza (Helsinki, Finland)
(24) Agency France Press
(25) Association of Independent Information Professionals
(26) Brain Bridge, Inc.
(27) Borska Group, Inc.

(28) e-Rewards Market Research
(29) Financial Times
(30) First-to-Know, Inc.
(31) First Rain, Inc.
(32) Global Insight
(33) Guideline
(34) Hoover's, Inc.
(35) ISI Emerging Markets
(36) Merger Market
(37) Mintel
(38) Metro City Design & Information Systems, Inc.
(39) nxt MOVE
(40) Penn Side Partners Ltd.
(41) Piers
(42) Power Capital Consulting
(43) Questel Orbit
(44) Reuters
(45) SciTech Strategies, Inc.
(46) Sheila Greco Associates
(47) Silobreakers Ltd. (London, UK)
(48) Special Libraries Association
(49) Strategy Software, Inc.
(50) The PRS Group
(51) The Wall Street Journal Online
(52) Vantage Point/Search Technology, Inc.
(53) Wincite Systems
(54) Caudra Associates, Inc.

3. The Curricula of Business Intelligence Education in France

In America, the Society of Competitive Intelligence Professionals (SCIP) was founded in 1986; while in France, SCIP France (Association Française pour la Promotion de l'Intelligence Economique) was founded by Robert Guillaumot in Paris. As will be seen below, SCIP France sparked off Intelligence Economique

(IE) research in various fields of industry, the government and academia.[1,2]

3.1. *IE in industry*

The activities of SCIP France gradually became widespread and permeated the business community in France. Robert Guillaumot founded Academie de l'I.E. in 1993, whose members include influential corporate people.[3] Ten years later in April 2002, based on

---

[1] About the French term "Intelligence Economique": the French word "intelligence" does not have the connotations of the English "intelligence," and the French equivalent is either "information" or "renseignement." As both are used as military terms, the English term must have been borrowed into the lexicon.

[2] Robert Guillaumot defines IE (business intelligence) thus:

> "The global economic environment surrounding corporations is now beset by diversified risks and destabilizing factors; yet it contains many business opportunities. What we propose is IE for corporate activities, which leads corporations towards success in this business environment. IE provides companies with know-how for promoting systems suited for companies of any size; collects, investigates, and analyzes information surrounding companies; and finds strategies and tactics best suited for them, and gives advice on how to put them into practice."

[3] Other than Robert Guillaumot, the membership is composed of IE experts of the French government, industry and academia; notably, Mr. Legendre, former board member and international chairperson of Syntec Informatique, president of Cognitis, and also member of Club de l'Intelligence Economique of MEDEF Paris; Mr. Libman, chairperson of SCIP France; Mr. Pepin, CIGREF committee member; and Mr. Gillyboeuf, a French army general.

Recent activities:

- Awarding prizes for books on IE.
- Holding an IE Day for French and European companies: MEDEF Paris published a leaflet titled "IE Promotion among Corporations," which gave high acclaim to the academy's activities in 2004, which fell on the academy's 10th anniversary. Since then, the academy has held an IE Day every other year.
- Promoting IE within and outside business by posting members' opinions about IE on the blog of a major French economic journal, *Les Echos*, which general readers can leave comments on.

the concepts of Institut pour le Developpement de l'Entreprise dans son Environnement (IDEE) which Guillaumot presided over along with the Academie, Cercle d'Intelligence Economique was founded as an internal organization of Mouvement des Entreprises de France (MEDEF Paris). With the objective of improving member companies (especially small to medium-sized organizations) in their abilities in future prediction, decision-making, competition, and risk management, by utilizing IE (business intelligence), Cercle d'Intelligence Economique created working groups within the branch to work on enhancement of IE effects within companies, issues faced by smaller businesses, and legal issues relating to IE activities.

An example of its strategies is the collaborative scheme between the military and business, where both parties exchange information and strategies, with not just smaller companies but many large corporations participating. MEDEF Paris signed a collaboration project charter, along with 15 other organizations and the French army. Through this collaboration project, 180,000 smaller businesses are enabled to enhance their potential; and they have benefited in defense against competitors by using the highly advanced information-processing tools that incorporate the military's know-how and techniques. Along with a retired army man who lives in Paris, Brice de Gliame, President of ITB — a member company of MEDEF Paris — is one of the promoters of this project, and has been active in promoting corporate defense against competitors both within and without France.[4]

The background of MEDEF Paris' decision to sign the charter is as follows. The necessity for defense in business had been widely recognized by both the military and the private sector as early as 1995,

---

[4]ITB was founded by executive officers of major corporations and information service companies, in order to provide advanced information and consulting services to companies. It specializes in offering innovative solutions and measures to companies that are becoming more defensive as competition grows fiercer.

Also, since the military and business have become allied, ITB has worked to seek effective measures through seeking experts' advice in various fields such as information technology, organization, security, human resource development, and both offensive and defensive IE, and also through studying the military know-how and techniques.

and the government also acknowledged the necessity for cooperation among companies, and the necessity for defense, security and IE for companies. Since the US and other countries had already adopted these measures, it was decided that France must immediately deal with this matter too, hence the decision to sign the project charter.

MEDEF Paris promotes this movement to industry associations in local cities. It also gives support to other organizations such as Club d'Intelligence Economique et Strategique, and Association Française pour le Developpement de l'Intelligence Economique (AFDIE).

Furthermore, a federation of local chambers of commerce, Association de Chambres Française de Commerce et de l'Industrieno, established a branch for IE and innovation — Direction de l'Innovation et de l'Intelligence Economique, headed by Philippe Clerc.[5] Thus, the IE movement became widespread in France.

This association of chambers of commerce has been active in promoting IE since late 2005, in response to the government's IE promotion initiative. The association's three-year plan, which is targeted mainly at management of smaller businesses, involves agenda such as those below:

- Follow the government's policies and the movement's progress;
- Keep track of industry information, developments and trends in general;
- Support the setting up of organizations for nationwide movements, and promote participation in international seminars and conferences;
- Give guidance on regional IE activities and support local activists;
- Promote mutual support for problem-monitoring activities, and construct networks for this purpose;
- Communicate principles and policies of cooperation among local chambers of commerce and their associations;
- Report the activities of Mouvement des Entreprises de France.

---

[5] There are 155 chambers of commerce in France; and above which, 20 regional chambers of commerce, with Association de Chambres Française de Commerce et de l'Industrieno at the top. There are also French chambers of commerce overseas, and business networks widespread in and outside of France.

3.2. *The government's IE promotion activities*

France lags approximately ten years behind America in IE activities, which aim to collect, analyze, and utilize effective strategic information for results in economic activities. Therefore, the French government formed a committee for Competitive Economic Security in 1995. In 2003 Deputy Bernard Carayon submitted a report on the importance of IE promotion, at the behest of the then prime minister, Jean Pierre Raffarin. Alain Juillet was appointed Haut responsable charge de l'intelligence economique au Secretariat generale de la defense nationale (SGDN) in the same year.[6] Nicolas Sarkozy, then Ministre d'Etat, and Ministre de l'Economie, des Finances et de l'Industrie, organized an IE branch (Delegation Generale de l'I.E.) in 2004. Thus, the IE movement in France has become gradually active.

3.3. *IE in the French academia*

In an interview he gave to an economic journal, *Le Journal du Management*, Alain Juillet said: "Nowadays, many business schools and universities in the world have IE programs, and there are many graduates who have received IE education. Therefore, they can easily apply what they learned to business when they join companies and have proven that they are superior to other employees in their business practice and decision-making. Also, they can predict future trends and events thanks to their IE education, which enables them to start preparing solutions, giving them a strong competitive edge.

---

[6]Alain Juillet is the most active promoter of IE in the French government, and is given the nickname of "Monsieur Intelligence Economique." Born in 1942, he received a degree and CPA certificate from Stanford University, after which he served as a paratroop officer for five years. From 1967 to 1982, he worked for Pernot-Ricard Group's international department, and subsequently worked in 63 countries as a corporate reconstruction, globalization, and crisis management specialist. This earned him the position of Direction générale de la sécurité extérieure (national security and information) in Ministre Française de la Défense in October 2003, and then the above-mentioned position of "haut responsable chargé de l'intelligence économique au secrétariat général de la défense nationale" (SGDN) in December 2003.

IE-enabled employees would be one effective way of advantageous management of business."

Undoubtedly partly due to his efforts as SGDN, there are now many educational institutions in France that offer IE programs. For example:

- Institut de la Communication et des Technologies Nouvelles (Vienne)
- Universite Toulouse 1 (Haute Garonne)
- Ecole Internationale des Sciences du Traitement de l'Information (Val d'Oise)
- Université Lyon 3
- Ecole Nationale Supereure d'Ingenieurs de Caen
- Ecole de Guerre Économique, Paris
- Ecole Européenne de l'Intelligence Economique, Versaille.

Among the schools mentioned above, Ecole de Guerre Economique was founded in 1997 in response to globalization of the economy, with the aim of providing future executives with IE strategy study, information risk management, and risk prediction training. In its one-year course, students learn how to defeat competitors; how to detect false reporting by media or rumors, and avoid being influenced by it; and how to conduct case studies of companies that have collapsed in management, and prevent such a fate. Students also conduct field studies of the risks involved in fraudulent activities in business transactions so as to learn the importance of preventing illegal activities and preserving corporate ethics through group studies, case studies, and analysis of competitive intelligence provided by companies. The school's alumni pursue careers as global corporate risk managers, analysts, and project managers, among others, in major corporations.

Ecole Européenne de l'Intelligence Economique is a graduate school that was founded as an IE specialist school in Versailles, 2006, by Benoit de Saint-Sernan and others who were involved in establishing Ecole de Guerre Économique. Its curriculum is as follows:

Basic theory and methods (400 hours)

Professional training course (1,200 hours)

With the objective of training future IE professionals in various businesses, 18 IE experts teach the following topics:

- Explanation of the actual work involved in working for a corporation, such as marketing, accounting, sales, communications, and administration, so that this knowledge will help future IE professionals in their work;
- Current affairs;
- IE among corporations;
- IE's role for corporations;
- Techniques for collection, analysis and selection of information necessary for IE;
- CRM;
- Statistics analysis;
- Communication strategy;
- Lobbying strategy;
- EU;
- Corporate defense: how to obtain necessary information;
- Crisis management;
- Risk management;
- How corporations may survive the Intelligence War.

In the unique practical case-study class, companies commission work to the graduate school, and students offer paid-service to companies, setting up systems to respond to their requests and to bear results. The merit of this class for the school and the students is that this keeps them in close contact with the companies, thus giving the students a higher possibility of employment upon graduation.[7]

Career assistance course (45 hours): 3 lecturers and 3 advisers
---
The school provides extra lectures and training classes when deemed necessary, depending on the results of level checks. Also, there is a

---

[7] The school's placement rate is said to be 85%.

career advice room on campus, which provides consulting services and offers to contact corporations on behalf of students.

Total hours: 1,645. Duration of the course: one year
Starting from October 15, 2008 to June 26, 2009.

Entrance requirements: university degrees, competency in a second language, English

The faculty consists of 18 members, including well-known figures in the IE field such as Alain Juillet, the French IE guru and IE officer who reports directly to the prime minister; François Jakobiak, emeritus professor at Université Libre de Bruxelles; and other IE experts experienced in security knowledge management, corporate strategy, crisis management, and small to medium business consultancy, and who have published books on these topics.

Another excellent characteristic of this school is its location. As it is located in the suburbs of Paris, a mere 16 km away and within 20 minutes' train ride, it gives easy access to major corporations in Paris, and to the European Commission, educational institutions in various EU countries, and companies outside of France. It is the school's primary objective to work in close cooperation with those organizations.

As noted above, the education the school offers is unique in that it offers students opportunities to learn not just IE theories but its practical usage, thus training them to be corporate experts. The school also supports students' future careers through close communication with companies.

As we have seen, France's IE movement is evenly distributed amongst the military, government, business and academia, and each field promotes IE in cooperation with others. Much may be learned from their example.

PART II

Chapter 7

Business Intelligence and Crisis Management — How Companies Reacted to Crises

1. Introduction

Since the 1700s, there have been four major earthquakes in the region surrounding Tokyo in Japan: the 1703 Genroku Earthquake, the 1782 Tenmei Earthquake, the 1855 Ansei Edo Earthquake, and the 1923 Great Kanto Earthquake. When we look at the intervals between these earthquakes, they are 79 years, 73 years and 68 years, respectively: an average of 73 years.

This has led to a theory that major earthquakes occur approximately every 70 years in this region. This theory cannot be said to have a strictly scientific basis as it builds on only four data points, but I will try to make a mathematical equation out of this.

If we create a linear regression model with the years as dependent variables and the number of earthquakes as independent variables, we have:

$$Y = 1632.5 + 73.7X.$$

To predict the next major earthquake, assign the value 5 to X. When we do that, we have $y = 1999$ as the year when the next major earthquake occurs. It is the year that Nostradamus foretold annihilation of the human race, and also the year when Japan would go bankrupt according to Professor Morimoto of Hakuoh University. Luckily, neither prediction came to pass.

The extreme scarcity of data in the formula above is a saving grace as it makes the prediction unreliable, but the correlation is, astonishingly, $r = 0.999$. Considering the average of the past records, and estimating from this simple predictive formula, the next Great Kanto Earthquake could happen any time now. Of course, it is one's individual choice whether or not to believe this prediction, and there is also no guarantee that the past cycle would necessarily be repeated in future. However, we may safely say that we should be on alert for the next major earthquake.

My motive in writing this chapter is that I have felt the need to review earthquakes from the perspectives of risk, crisis management and contingency plans, as their range and diversity have broadened. Risk and crisis management lie in the area of knowledge management in that they involve obtaining, sharing and using knowledge (business intelligence); at the same time, they also lie in the genres of knowledge science and engineering, where they should be developed into social systems for disaster prevention and safety measures.

There is no perfect fundamental counter-disaster measure; we must make continual efforts. We must grasp the potential damage by simulating what would happen if a major earthquake of the magnitude of the Great Hanshin Earthquake or the Mid-Niigata Earthquake were to occur during the day on a weekday, and explore measures at an individual level, an organizational level, and a national level.

First, we define "emergency" or "contingency" (see Table 2). Following that, we will look at some real-life cases and discuss how we can establish crisis management systems, and the necessity for continual simulated training and practical approaches, and for establishing proactive measures and emergency measures.

Table 2: Categories of Contingencies and Their Examples

1. Political unrest
   a) Disbanding of the ruling party, or its power waning
   b) Frequent occurrences of international or domestic terrorism
   c) Resignation of the Cabinet, or dissolution of the ruling party due to election results
   d) Assassination of political leaders

2. Economic unrest
   a) Extreme fluctuation of major currencies
   b) Extreme fluctuation of the official discount rate
   c) Extreme change in financial or monetary policies
   d) Sudden drop in public bonds' credit
   e) Extreme decrease in public and private investment
   f) Considerable drop in consumer spending
   g) Increase in the unemployment rate
   h) Shortage of raw materials
   i) Drop in general economic indicators
   j) Economic sanction
   k) Worsening of the subprime mortgage crisis

3. Social unrest
   a) Lack of leaders
   b) Shortage of workforce
   c) Lengthening strikes in the public sector or major private sector companies
   d) Expansion of excessively aggressive consumer movement
   e) Expansion of disparity in wealth (disappearance of middle-class)
   f) Extreme measures for eliminating employment discrimination
   g) Serious diseases — e.g., outbreaks of epidemics, AIDS, Avian influenza, and anthrax disease
   h) Increase in suicides
   i) Acceleration of global warming
   j) Increased desertification
   k) Shortage of water

4. Military unrest
   a) Intrusion into territorial waters or airspace by a potential threat
   b) Amassment of troops on a large scale near the border
   c) Failure of a military treaty
   d) Failure in negotiation on national security matters
   e) A third country moving into a (potential) war zone
   f) Considerable amendment to a security treaty
   g) Extreme fortifying of a neighboring nation's military strength
   h) Accelerated proliferation of nuclear weapons

(Continued)

Table 2:   (*Continued*)

---

5. Legal unrest
   a) Extreme tightening of antitrust law or privatization-related bills
   b) Sudden amendment to Customs Act
   c) Excessive strengthening of Consumer Protection Act
   d) Extreme regulation of products or production process by Environmental Act
   e) Inadequate application of Workers' Compensation Act

6. International unrest
   a) Sudden hike in oil (and other vital raw materials') prices
   b) Emergence of protectionism for resources and technologies
   c) Rapid increase in regulations of free trade
   d) Intensification of competition against developing countries
   e) Disruption in foreign investment and import markets
   f) Plummeting of property prices

7. Changes in technology
   a) Emergence of extreme protectionism
   b) Increase in patent disputes
   c) Extreme increase or decrease in technological disparity
   d) Broadening of technological disparity between developed and developing countries

8. Natural disaster
   a) Major earthquakes
   b) Typhoons, cyclones, and hurricanes
   c) Massive flooding
   d) Damage brought on by abnormal weather phenomena such as windstorms and flood damage, drought, and shortage of water
   e) Local rainstorms

9. Industrial unrest
   a) Collapse of stable markets
   b) Price collapse, or unstable market price
   c) Rollout of new definitive products by competitors
   d) Product liability lawsuits on a large scale
   e) Powerful competitors entering the market
   f) Merger and acquisition by competitors
   g) Organizational restructuring of competitors
   h) Massive drop in domestic demand
   i) Sudden big change in consumer activities
   j) Forceful implementation of inappropriate policies
   k) Widespread false labeling
   l) Inappropriate contaminants in products

(*Continued*)

Table 2: (*Continued*)

10. Internal unrest
   a) Cancellation of order from the most important client
   b) Failure of a big project where a large-scale order was expected
   c) Weakening of brands in major markets
   d) Serious defects in products (including containers and raw materials)
   e) Serious defects in information systems
   f) Fire or explosion in factories and facilities
   g) Theft of major products and raw materials
   h) Problems with debts or fundraising
   i) Kidnapping of executives
   j) Bankruptcy of affiliated or client companies
   k) Aggravation of employees' strikes
   l) Aggravation of strikes at supplier or client companies
   m) Radioactive leak in nuclear facilities
   n) Destruction of nuclear facilities

Source: Akira Ishikawa, *Strategic Budget Management*, Dobunkan, pp. 139–140.

2. Necessity for Establishing Crisis Management Systems, Continual Simulated Training and Practical Approaches

2.1. *IBM's case*

We must be prepared for crises and emergencies, even in peacetime. We should have regular emergency drills and establish practical programs. During the Great Hanshin Earthquake, many companies and local governments proved unprepared for the disaster, but there were companies that managed to set up relief activities. What was the difference between them?

IBM Japan had an Emergency Plan in place at 5.47 a.m., on January 17, 1995 — just one minute after the magnitude-7.2 earthquake shook the Hanshin region.

The news of the earthquake first reached Isao Kato, then general manager of customer service department, IBM Kawasaki Higashi office in Kawasaki. The news was immediately reported to the president, Kakutaro Kitashiro, and an emergency headquarters was set up an hour and 14 minutes later at 7 a.m., with Kitashiro installed as the chief.

Meanwhile, the Hanshin headquarters was based in Dojima, Osaka. Noriyuki Yoshiyasu, the Kansai region technical manager, was appointed as chief of the Hanshin emergency team.

IBM Japan did not know much about what was happening in the area yet, but the company secured trucks first and began preparing to send materials for restoration efforts. A shortage of manpower was likely, even though there were 600 engineers in the Kansai Region Engineering Department, as many employees fell victim to the earthquake which occurred before they left home for work. With transport and electricity out as well, reinforcement team members were enlisted, mainly from those who had experience of working in Kobe, but also from branches all over Japan. The reinforcement teams from Sapporo and Tokyo flew to Osaka, while those from Nagoya and Kyushu drove.

IBM Japan already had Special Assignment Teams of 10 people each, which stood by round-the-clock in Tokyo and Osaka for system maintenance of nationwide clients. Most clients' computers had the auto-call system for emergency. Thus, when the earthquake occurred, IBM immediately knew there was considerable damage in the areas surrounding Kobe and Osaka. It was able to set the emergency plan into motion quickly, as the plan had been well-drilled through training in peacetime.

There were 45 large and mid-range IBM computers, respectively, used in companies and government offices in the Hanshin region, and over 1,000 systems that clients used, not even counting PC networks. Thankfully, the restoration support system was set up by the late afternoon of the 17th, and IBM began restoring systems in order of priority. If the systems related to lifelines such as transport and electricity had not been recovered immediately, secondary disasters could have spread. In many cases, the earthquake caused equipment to fall to the floor, and two mainframe computers had to be entirely replaced.

IBM had experienced natural disasters in various parts of the world before, including the Los Angeles Earthquake in the US. Directly after the Hanshin Earthquake occurred in Japan, relief teams in the US, Germany, France, Italy, the UK and Canada started preparing to send engineers and equipment to Japan. Meanwhile, teams in Korea and Taiwan were on high alert. It is true that computer makers do have systems to respond to all sorts of problems that their customers may have, though not necessarily related to natural disasters. Yet, it has to be said that IBM's initial efforts did facilitate restoration work later on. Knowledge was indeed turned into intelligence in this case.

IBM's crisis management manual, called the Disaster Plan, is not specifically for earthquakes or different types of disasters. Japanese companies are actually ahead of IBM when it comes to having detailed manuals for earthquakes that even provide counter-measures according to earthquake magnitude. However, once emergencies occur, there is no time to consult detailed manuals; we need to act on the spot. As general manager Kato pointed out, "The real issue is whether or not the company has established a system where people can act quickly and effectively."

In IBM Japan's case, the emergency headquarters chief Kitashiro had Kato of the emergency team report directly to him, and delegated power to Kato as the person in charge of the situation. Kitashiro gave Kato "extralegal" authority to procure goods and manpower for restoration work without having to ask for permission. Thus, without the hassle of going through internal bureaucracy, IBM was able to act quickly.

The emergency headquarters also gave as much authority as possible to Yoshiyasu, the Hanshin headquarters chief. By having separate "Emergency Headquarters" and "Hanshin Headquarters," IBM managed to make calm, objective judgments in dealing with the disaster. When it appeared that restoration work might be under way, IBM published an internal letter relating to "Customer care in the Hanshin Earthquake restoration efforts" on July 20, and reiterated to employees that its priority was restoration so that they would not think of this as a business opportunity.

IBM's manual is not a desk plan; it reflects lessons learnt from actual disasters. It contains a volume of data regarding the 1994 Northridge Earthquake, the 1994 Sanriku Earthquake, and the 1993 Southern Kyushu Flood, including records of damages and actual measures taken. Emergency teams in various countries are required to watch video clips of the damage that natural disasters can cause to computer equipment. For example, Kato had watched the footage of the Northridge Earthquake.

IBM acts quickly in a crisis, even in the initial stages when the extent of damage is unclear. It firmly believes that even if its actions turn out to be needless later on, it must act first and think later. Even if it turns out that the company has been overreacting, its employees will nevertheless have gained valuable experience and training.

2.2. *The Asahi Breweries Group's case*

Asahi's Tokyo Factory [closed down in 2002] has a fire-safety scheme in cooperation with the local fire department and the local community; in case of fire caused by earthquakes, the factory workers would help with extinguishing the fire in its initial stage, and with administering first aid. This is called the Community Disaster Support Team Scheme, a disaster relief scheme founded in 1990, separate from the "fire defense organization for self-protection" (community fire brigade) that is required by the Fire Service Act.

Asahi's Community Disaster Support Team consists of 260 Tokyo Factory workers, mainly in their 20s and 30s. The headquarters has 20 members, and there are 48 taskforce groups of five. Thus, half of the 550 employees that are in the premises would be engaged in fire-safety operations. The area they are responsible for is approximately 550 meters radius of the factory, which includes an old residential area on the south side. The group would be under the command of the community fire brigade. As the community has an aging population, many of the fire brigade members are now over 70, so they welcome younger people's participation in the communal efforts for disaster prevention.

Taskforce members carry backpacks that contain "the seven tools": a torch, a sling, a pair of gloves, an armband and a first-aid manual, among others. They also have stretchers. Each team has five members so that there is one extra person to act freely even when four people are carrying a stretcher.

Of course, it is a difficult task even for professional firemen to extinguish a fire and rescue people in the chaos of a fire caused by an earthquake. For the laymen to do that, they would have to train quite seriously on a regular basis. Therefore, when the Community Disaster Support Team scheme commenced in the summer of 1990, about 85 members participated in training and received careful instruction from the local Omori Fire Department's rescue squad members. The training was recorded on video for the absent or future members.

During the annual Ohta-ward disaster drills, the group trains in firefighting and rescue work under the instruction of the Fire Department. The factory also holds an Advanced Emergency Aid Skill Workshop in collaboration with the Ohta-ward Fire Department. This nine-hour class consists of lectures and training. The Tokyo Fire Department issues certificates to those who finish the workshop, and more than 40 people have received certificates so far.

Along with such physical support, Asahi provides the community with water for extinguishing fires or for drinking. According to the accord with the Ohta-ward office, Asahi is to provide 3,000 tons of water from the 4,000-ton water tank for brewing beer.

Kyoji Makita, administrative manager of the Tokyo Factory, who championed the Community Disaster Support Team scheme, says he felt the local community's high expectations for the relief team when he attended a community meeting after the Great Hanshin Earthquake. However, he thinks that simultaneous multiple fires like those in Kobe would be beyond the team's control once the fires were to start in earnest. Therefore, initial response is vital.

Ideally, each family should have a fire-extinguisher at home, and leave it outside the house when there is a fire in the neighborhood. That would help initial fire-fighting efforts, as the support team or the local fire brigade could collect them to use at the site. There are 350 fire-extinguishers in the Tokyo Factory, which would be used to put out fires outside the factory facilities too.

It would be difficult and hazardous to rescue people who are buried under a collapsed building without the appropriate tools to lift up heavy weights. Yet, if the team member calls out to the victim,

"I'm with Asahi's rescue support team. Help is near," it may give the victim some moral support.

According to Asahi, there is no employee within the company who is reluctant to join the rescue support team. That may be so, but some employees must feel that they would rather run to their families than save the community or the factory, if they are being completely honest with themselves. If more companies started to contribute to the community relief and rescue efforts, and if it was commonly accepted that your family would be protected by the local company, it would help to lessen such anxiety.

There are hardly any other examples like Asahi's, however, where a rescue support system is established, although other companies do offer help in case of fire in the neighborhood, such as Suntory's Musashino Factory. Therefore, there is a need for stronger incentives for corporate communal contribution, which is an important genre of BI activities.

3. Establishing Proactive Measures and Emergency Measures

The term "contingencies" refers to unthinkable events happening in real life. Unexpected situations can occur one after another, and quite often, the government and other institutions related to disaster prevention do not know what to do at a time like this.

There are three basic attitudes towards contingencies, where the unthinkable becomes reality. Firstly, the most passive of the three, the fatalistic attitude: giving it up as a lost cause. During the Great Hanshin Earthquake, out of the 195 patients who were brought into Higashi Kobe Hospital in Higashi Nada ward in Kobe City immediately after the earthquake, 73 people (38%) died just before they reached the hospital. Their fate was decided within the first few minutes after the earthquake. Nearly half the people died without ever receiving any medical treatment.

The second attitude involves attempting to establish a system which would enhance the chance of surviving contingencies even a little, instead of leaving it up to fate; this school of thought first draws up an action plan in order of priority, and then creates a manual for contingencies. That is what the US Federal Emergency Management Agency did.

3.1. *The Federal Emergency Management Agency (FEMA)*

The US Federal Emergency Management Agency (FEMA) was established against contingencies during the Carter administration in 1992. Headquartered in Washington, it has over 2,600 staff members who work in directorates such as Recovery, Disaster Operations, Mitigation, National Preparedness, and the US Fire Administration and other offices. There are also ten regional operations in major cities such as Boston, Philadelphia, Atlanta, Chicago, San Francisco, and Seattle. Where there is a contingency situation, about 4,000 experts will be mobilized. FEMA is in command of 28 federal agencies in its comprehensive emergency management to protect people's lives, assets, and organizations from all hazards.

FEMA reported the Northridge Earthquake to President Clinton within 15 minutes after the occurrence, which enabled the president to make timely decisions on important matters and announce the measures to be taken on the same day. In contrast, in the case of the Great Hanshin Earthquake, Prime Minister Murakami reportedly was not notified of the gravity of the situation until the afternoon of the day of the earthquake.

By reporting directly to the president, FEMA acted promptly in disaster management; however, it was demoted after the US Department of Homeland Security was founded following 9/11 in 2001. As a consequence, when Hurricane Katrina made landfall in August 2005, FEMA's response came under criticism, leading to the resignation of FEMA director Michael D. Brown.

One year later, New Orleans's population was still less than half of the previous population of 460,000 before the disaster, which put it at the level of 1880. About one-third of rubble was still not cleared away. Sixty percent of residents still did not have access to electricity. Only 17% of buses were running. Six out of nine hospitals in the city were closed, and the suicide rate was three times higher than before the disaster. This data shows the difficulties involved in uphill work reconstruction.

The third attitude, of the three basic attitudes towards contingencies mentioned earlier, is to predict various contingencies and minimize the damage as much as possible.

3.2. The case of Corporation A

Oil company A is headquartered in a 52-storey skyscraper in the center of Los Angeles. Escape routes are limited to the staircase or the elevators, and if those routes are cut off, employees will be trapped inside the building.

When an earthquake triggers the collapse of a highway or multiple fires, it is highly likely that rescue teams may not be sent immediately to the building. Given that there are about 900 people who work there, each of the floors has therefore been stocked with enough food and water to last three days. Also, each floor has flashlights, radio transceivers, and medical supplies. In addition, Corporation A has set up its own Emergency Center, apart from the regular security center, and has assigned safety control specialists.

When the magnitude-6.6 Northridge Earthquake occurred in Los Angeles on January 17, 1994, severe damage was sustained by highways, bridges and public buildings. Steel-framed skyscrapers that had previously been considered resilient against earthquakes, had welding parts cracked by the earthquake. One skyscraper appeared to have survived the earthquake unscathed. However, a later investigation revealed many cracks in the welding, and the building needed reinforcement work at an estimated cost of one billion yen.

It is not wise to assume contingencies will never happen. We must predict all hazards, and eliminate possible causes as much as possible.

3.3. The case of Daiei Group

When major earthquakes strike out of the blue, the actual damage sustained in the disaster areas is usually not reported in the initial stages. It is a test of true leadership and management skills for government and corporate leaders, whether they can make accurate estimations to protect victims' safety and lives, and provide them with necessary food and water promptly.

Daiei Group's Vice President Jun Nakauchi reportedly arrived at the company's headquarters in Hamamatsu at 6.20 a.m. on January 17, 1995, within one hour after the occurrence of the Great Hanshin Earthquake. Executive director Kazuo Kawa arrived at nearly the same time, and a few staffers had already started trying to get in touch with colleagues from other Daiei branches.

Executive director Kawa was sent to the disaster area as the chief of the relief team, and his helicopter was allowed to land in Port Island, Kobe, at 1.45 p.m. on the same day. The relief team arrived in Harborland at 3 p.m., after flying over the Kobe Bridge which had a one-meter gap in the center as joints had come off.

As was expected, the telephone service was disrupted. In anticipation of this, the headquarters had borrowed mobile satellite communications equipment. The mobile maritime satellite communications service, Inmarsat, arrived by six in the evening, thus enabling the relief team to have detailed communication with the headquarters.

It should also be noted that before executive director Kawa and the nine other relief team members left Tokyo by helicopters, the helicopters were loaded with 1,000 meals. Daiei did what it could do at that time proactively, by anticipating what would be needed in the aftermath of the earthquake.

Daiei took proactive measures successively, after its immediate initial response. First, on top of sending emergency food by helicopters, it sent a ferry from the Port of Fukuoka. This ferry, however, was not bound for the Port of Kobe but for the Port of Izumi Otsu, Osaka, as Daiei had received information that the Port of Kobe was closed due to the extensive damage it had sustained.

The ferry was loaded with portable gas stoves, food, and two tankers carrying water. These water tankers were arranged by executive director Kawa, when the Tokyo headquarters had first made the decision at eight in the morning to send supplies. Although the level

An Introduction to Knowledge Information Strategy

of damage to the lifelines was not yet confirmed, Kawa had proactively decided to provide free drinking water. Not only that, he also gave an order to send another tanker by land from Fukuoka to Kobe, in case the ferry did not arrive.

Daiei further sent 20,000 umbrellas, 12,000 portable raincoats, 10,000 raincoats, 15,000 rainwear, 6,000 plastic raincoats, and 20,000 tarpaulins from the Kobe distribution center to branches that were re-opened on January 21, when heavy rain was predicted. This was another example of its proactive measures to save the evacuees from further discomfort and misery.

3.4. *The case of West Japan Railway Company*

Today, many global and multinational companies have more than three headquarters in Japan, Europe, America and other places. The main reason for this is that a decentralized system is more resilient and flexible, and enables companies to react more promptly to the different regions than a centralized system. Another important reason, however, is dispersion of risk.

In a country like Japan that is frequently beset by disasters, both man-made and natural (e.g., the Aum cult's Sarin Gas Attack, earthquakes and typhoons), it is not surprising if companies decide to have three headquarters within the nation for the sake of risk dispersion.

In fact, Masataka Ide, the former president of West Japan Railway Company, noted that the company would not be able to function in an emergency if the Osaka headquarters were to shut down, unless a system is set up so that branches in Kobe and Kyoto can also function as headquarters. This includes not just installing backup systems for a computer-assisted traffic control system, but also establishing secure fiber-optic network systems for alternative lines.

This is still not sufficient, however; according to Ide, it is problematic from the perspective of risk dispersion that many officers live in the same remote area, distant from the headquarters. He argued that officers should have more than one house in diverse areas, and for some positions it is even necessary to have officers live in designated areas. Thus, the multiple-headquarters system is not only about having headquarters overseas; the necessity for such a system within the same nation has been on the rise in recent years.

3.5. *Crisis management system for personal computers*

In the aftermath of the Great Hanshin Earthquake, many organizations have seriously debated installing CP and crisis management manuals, and progress has been made in that area. It is clear, though, that this is not enough.

First of all, crisis management manuals have to be distributed to all members of an organization, and must be carefully studied by them. Just handing out the manuals is not enough. Staff must be thoroughly familiar with the content, so that they can act accordingly in times of emergency.

It is also necessary to conduct written tests and simulated drills on a regular basis, to test employees' understanding of manuals and their ability to act on them. As it is, their test scores are usually far below the expected level in crisis management tests.

This again, however, is not enough. Crisis management information systems for computers need to be developed, introduced, and their effectiveness assessed. Such information systems would enable companies to grasp the damage quickly, report it to the relevant departments, deploy personnel to the appropriate departments, and give instructions for evacuation; in other words, it facilitates implementation of the crisis management manual.

For example, Corporation E's crisis management system for computers includes products that have databases, map information, communications, and damage modeling. With these systems that offer useful, comprehensive information, photographs of the actual disaster sites can be sent digitally, the damage can be simulated, instructions for personnel assignment and evacuation can be given, and information about related facilities can be obtained.

4. Do Your Best and God Will Do the Rest

In an article titled "Danger Past, God Forgotten?" in the 6th edition of *Crisis Management Study: Annual Report* (March 1998), I pointed out the critically low budget for Research and Development (R&D) for Science and Technology Related to Disaster Management, the abominable lack of consideration for introducing crisis management programs in educational institutions, and the lack of interest among academics and professionals in establishing crisis management systems and their operations. I argued that these matters needed to be addressed. Since then, however, I am afraid the situation has been aggravated rather than improved.

As I have noted in this chapter, we tend to delay thinking about emergency and disaster measures, as our day-to-day business is more than enough to keep us occupied. This leads us to accept contingencies as a matter of fate, which in turn only leads to more deaths and loss of property. We must not spare any effort in actively studying the various types of contingencies, and in developing measures that would allow us to avoid such crises in the first place or that would help us deal with emergencies effectively. Our motto should be "Do your best and God will do the rest," rather than "Danger past, God forgotten."

5. Suggestions for Crisis Management that Makes Intelligent Use of BI

5.1. *Introduction*

First of all, we must question whether Japan has an "intelligent" society, both in its state management and in its crisis management. In regards to intellectual property, which is a product of an intellectual society, the Japanese patent system was only established a century later than in America; and according to Hisamitsu Arai, Japan lags behind America by more than 20 years in intellectual property strategy.

One proof of that can be seen in disputes over patents and inventions, which are part of BI. In the Hitachi patent dispute, the inventor was granted 1,630 million yen (71 times higher than the original payment); while in the blue LED invention dispute, the inventor was granted 20 billion yen (one million times higher than the original payment). These rulings of the Tokyo High Court and the district court only go to show that products of intelligent society, such as patents and inventions, are not given their proper value in Japan.

The same can be said of part-time lecturers in universities, which are supposedly the foundation of an intelligent society. Even if you have been lecturing for decades and have written dozens of books and hundreds of papers, your wage is hardly any different from that of a young, new part-time lecturer with almost no academic experience. Generally, once you step down from being a full-time lecturer to a part-time one, the wage value is cut down to less than one-tenth.

There are endless examples like this. It cannot be denied that our attempts at making use of IT fail because our society is, simply, not intelligent. I will hereafter discuss the prerequisites for intelligent use of IT in crisis management, as suggestions that do not satisfy prerequisites are merely academic.

5.2. *Futile crisis management*

Researchers of earthquakes unanimously and incessantly proclaim on television and in newspapers and magazines that major earthquakes in the Tokai region, the Nankai region, and the Kanto region can happen again any time now. The top priority of national leaders is to protect people's lives and property and to promote their happiness, and it is our duty, not just of leaders but every single one of us, to make utmost efforts to achieve this.

Yet, there is no sign of crisis management being incorporated into primary or secondary education as an obligatory subject. Furthermore, crisis management training on a regular basis is hardly conducted anywhere in this country. With crisis management training and education in such a deplorable state, this situation hardly invites our confidence or hope.

Such total neglect of this important issue in the government and academia affects distribution of resources too. According to the *1995 White Paper on Disaster Management* — the year of the Great

Hanshin Earthquake — although the Disaster Management Budget was over three trillion yen including loans, the budget for R&D for Science and Technology was 37.3 billion yen, which was a mere 1.125% of the total Disaster Management Budget. This shows the lack of interest in disaster prevention research that protects people's lives and property.

The government's priority of policies is thus irrational, and intellectual property has not been given its proper value yet in this society.

5.3. *Futile IT strategy*

The fifth-generation computer project that was initiated in Japan in the beginning of the 1980s shook the US federal government and the global computer industry. Naturally, there was an expectation that Japanese computers and communication networks would lead the world market. Many young researchers who should have become world-class science and engineering experts jumped into this genre. Now, a quarter of a century later, however, the project has been closed down. What happened?

Japan was also expected to lead the world in space engineering and development of space technology, as well as in information and telecommunications. In the former case, Japan's budget for space technology was one-digit lower than NASA's, and there were many failures, even some embarrassing ones in recent years. These failures highlighted deficiencies not just in Japan's IT technology and strategy, but also in its crisis management system. Even in information and telecommunications, Japan has gradually fallen behind Korea. Science and engineering majors in universities are increasingly dwindling nowadays.

Openness is crucial for IT strategy, but Japan does not have a university open to the world in the world language, English, as in the cases of the British Open University and the American University of Phoenix. Whereas these universities are certified by at least one of multiple licensing institutes, in Japan there is only one such university, the Open University of Japan, where tuition is mainly conducted in

Japanese. Also, there is only one licensing institute in Japan for distance learning for overseas students (the Ministry of Education, Culture, Sports, Science and Technology). This hardly enables Japan to respond resiliently to the rapidly changing scene of IT education and strategy, never mind being the leading force in the genre.

5.4. *Crisis management via intelligent use of IT*

In order to remedy the problems discussed above, we need to set a time limit and work on fundamental reform of frameworks for public administration, legislation, judiciary, science and technology, and society.

Japan's strength in IT lies in its total budget for research and in its number of researchers, which are second only to the US, and even above those of Germany, France and the UK combined (Research budget: Japan, 16 trillion yen; the total of the three nations, 12.6 trillion yen. Number of researchers: Japan, 660,000; the total of the three nations, 580,000. Source: *2002 White Paper*).

Furthermore, approximately 39,000 industrial robots are used in Japan, which implies the power of IT to some extent. Japan produces 52% of the world's industrial robots, four times more than the US. The main founding members of the RoboCup, which is an equivalent of the Olympic Games for robots, are Japanese researchers; they first started the scheme with the goal of competing in the FIFA World Cup in 2050.

Considering these factors, if we make fundamental changes to the system of research assessments and funds distribution, and apply state-of-the-art robot technology to space development, especially to development of large stationary platforms, it might contribute towards developing a crisis management system.

Japan has proven its excellence in the field of remote-controlled robots by putting them into practical use; for example, the use of remote-controlled robots in monitoring Mount Unzen-Fugen. Even if it does take a few seconds for radio waves to travel from the Earth to the moon, future construction on the moon by remote-control is quite possible, as the Japan Aerospace Exploration Agency had previously succeeded in its experiment of building a construct on a satellite from the Earth by remote-control in 1997.

This would mean that by remote-control of robot/manned-space machines that are installed on the large stationary platforms, we would be able to predict not just natural disasters such as earthquakes, tsunamis and volcano eruptions, but also human disasters such as acts of terrorism, regional conflicts and hijacking, and take effective measures, greatly enhancing the possibility of protecting human life and property. Furthermore, as more platforms are deployed and more cooperation among them is achieved, the feed-forward function will be enhanced, and as synergistic effects multiply, I believe it will greatly contribute to protection of human life and property not just in Japan but across the entire world, and to co-existence and co-prosperity of the entire human race.

5.5. *Conclusion*

In order to achieve such goals, we must spare no effort in striving to excel, especially in the genres of epistemology, ontology, teleology, and etymology; and in increasing the opportunities to utilize the best brains in the world in a value-adding manner. It has often been the case in Japan that initially vigorous large-scale projects gradually lose their dynamism, only to dwindle away in 20 to 30 years.

I believe that establishing a super-long-term value addition assessment system is the key to success of this project, and something that we can leave behind to the next generation with pride. At its core are the best human resource networks in the world, which cannot be built in a day.

Chapter 8

Environmental Issues and Crisis Management*

1. Introduction

Dr. Hideo Itokawa, an authority on rocketry who passed away in 1999, predicted in his last book, *Would the Human Race Be Annihilated in the 21st Century!?* (1994), that "Humankind is destined to be wiped off from the face of the earth within 50 years, just like mammoths in the past." In order to avoid this catastrophe, he proposed what is called "Population Theory" — a theory of propagating altruistic love instead of egotistical love. Unfortunately, he passed away before his theory was completed.

While somewhat more optimistic than Dr. Itokawa's theory, Dr. Junichi Nishizawa, recipient of the Order of Culture and president of Tokyo Metropolitan University, co-authored with Dr. Isao Ueno a similar book titled *Humankind Will Become Extinct in the Next Eighty Years*, in February 2000. The nucleus of this book is that while it is predicted that it will take another 150 years for carbon dioxide concentrations to reach the lethal 3% level where people will suffocate to death, as methane hydrate, which had been stable at the bottom of the sea, is becoming more and more unstable, it is highly likely that this will trigger the "Devil's Cycle" of methane and carbon dioxide, considerably escalating carbon dioxide concentrations.

---

*This chapter is adapted from the article in *Annals of Crisis Management Research*, No. 10, May 2002, pp. 1–5.

Therefore, it is not so erroneous a prediction to say that humankind will be exterminated in about 80 years from now.

Dr. Lester Brown, director of the Worldwatch Institute — a renowned American environmental think-tank — reports that the atmospheric carbon dioxide level has now reached the highest level in the past 150,000 years, and that most of the 232 species of primates that are closest to human beings among the mammalia are on the brink of extinction. Furthermore, approximately 10,000 people are starving to death everyday on earth, and about one billion people who live on the sterile lands in the African and Asian continents are barely surviving day-to-day.

The Herald Tribune published a summary of the IPCC panel's 1,000-page report on climate change on January 23, 2001. Well over 500 specialists and professionals were involved in drawing up this report. It is generally considered to be the most comprehensive analysis and evaluation of the earth's climate change situation. Notably, the report gave 5.8 degrees Celsius as the highest average temperature increase in 100 years from now, which is considerably higher than the 3.5 degrees Celsius estimated in a previous analysis. Consequently, sea levels are predicted to rise as high as 90 meters, which would not be so different from sea levels of 100 million years ago. The climate change in the next 100 years is likely to entail far graver consequences than that of the past 10,000 years, which may constitute a strong basis for the theories of humankind's imminent extinction mentioned above.

In the face of such grave environmental issues, effective crisis management is needed urgently as never before, on a global scale.

2. Public Hazard Issues and Environmental Risk

We become aware of the fact that environmental issues have arisen when corporate activities, especially manufacturing and the fruit of their activities — products — harm our lives, properties, and health, and when our living conditions deteriorate.

When such environmental issues emerge, companies are liable for the damage, which constitutes environmental risk for them. Moreover, if the soil is polluted to the extent that groundwater is contaminated in violation of the environmental laws, the offending companies bear the risk of being liable to administrative penalties or criminal charges, even if there is no actual damage to the community.

As environmental laws become more stringent, companies' environmental risks become higher, and they have to make bigger investments in preventative measures. Quite a few corporations have gone bankrupt because they could not afford to secure funds for preventative measures and litigation risks.

What is notable here is that the term "environmental issues" refers to two different phenomena both before and after the mid-1980s. Until the early 1980s, the principal offenders of environmental issues were mainly private companies; "environmental issues" meant pollution problems caused by corporate activities. Therefore, their causes were easy to identify, and they could be dealt with as local problems.

After the late 1980s, however, environmental issues became a serious matter of survival for the entire planet. Apart from industrial and urban pollution problems, other complex global issues such as global warming, ozone depletion, destruction of forests, desertification, acid rain and marine pollution came to pose serious threats to our survival.

When we say "environmental issues," therefore, it is not a simple, local matter for a single company or conglomerates, but for the entire country, the entire world, and the entire eco-system. Unless we take fundamental measures on these levels, environmental issues will not be solved.

3. Crisis Management Regulations for Global Environmental Issues

In this section, we will examine major cases of crisis management from the perspective of global environmental issues.

3.1. *Events relating to global warming*

1988: The Intergovernmental Panel on Climate Change (IPCC) was established, co-sponsored by the United Nations Environment Program and World Meteorological Organization.

1994: At the United Nations Conference on Environment and Development (UNCED), the United Nations Framework Convention on Climate Change (UNFCCC) was signed by 163 countries including Japan, and it became effective in 1994.

1995: The first UNFCCC Conference of Parties (COP1) was held in Berlin; however, it failed to conclude an emissions control policy on global warming, and forming of a concrete plan was postponed to 1997. While the Netherlands and other EU countries attempted to enforce stringent emissions control, the US and Australia, whose economy is characterized by high oil consumption, opposed them. Oil-producing nations supported the US and Australia, for fear of loss in oil demand.

1997: 161 countries participated in COP3 in Kyoto, Japan. After a series of negotiations, the Kyoto Protocol was adopted. Figure 4 shows COP3 major countries' carbon dioxide reduction targets.

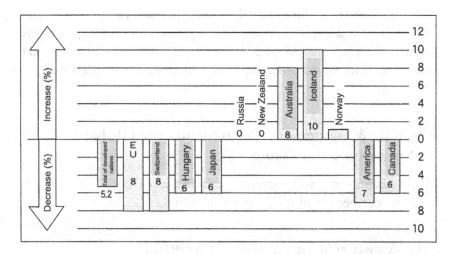

Figure 4:   COP3 Nations' Carbon Dioxide Reduction Targets

Source: The Environment Agency ("Nikkan Kogyo Shimbun" — Business & Technology Daily News, February 16, 1999).

1998: At COP4 held in Buenos Aires, Argentina, the host nation, Argentina, submitted a proposal to encourage developing countries to join the Convention voluntarily. However, 19 developing countries rejected it and only two decided to join it. (Further developments will be discussed in Section 4.)

3.2. *Events relating to the ozone depletion*

1985: The Vienna Convention for the Protection of the Ozone Layer was adopted in Vienna, Austria; the parties agreed to a 50% reduction of the ozone-depleting substances (ODSs) such as chlorofluorocarbons (CFC) and halons within the next ten years. To supplement the Vienna Convention, the Montreal Protocol on Substances That Deplete the Ozone Layer was concluded in 1987, which prescribes regulatory action plans for various ODSs.

1989: The Helsinki Declaration was adopted at the first conference of the parties to the Montreal Protocol; it called for a phase-out of CFCs and halons by 2000, tightening the timetable agreed upon in the Montreal Protocol.

1992: ODS-control measures were further tightened; the ban was accelerated by four years and specified CFCs and specified halons, along with three other ODSs, were to be eliminated by 1996.

3.3. *Events relating to acid rain*

1979: Acid rain is caused by sulfur oxides and nitrogen oxides in long-distance, cross-border air pollution. Therefore, the Convention on Long-Range Transboundary Air Pollution was concluded, with the United Nations Economic Commission for Europe (UNECE) as its principal body, though initially the issue was raised by OECD.

1985: The next phase was emission reduction of each pollutant. Firstly, the Protocol on the Reduction of Sulfur Emissions was concluded in Helsinki, Finland.

1988: Secondly, the Protocol on the Control of Nitrogen Oxides was concluded in Sophia, Bulgaria.

1995: It was discovered that one of the causes for acid rain in Japan was quite likely cross-border air pollution from Southeast Asia brought on by the monsoon, according to research by the Agency of the Environment and the Research Institute of Innovative Technology for the Earth. Accordingly, the Agency of the Environment proposed to 10 southeastern countries the construction of a Southeast Asia acid rain network for monitoring acid rain.

3.4. *Events relating to forest destruction*

1992: "The Statement of Principles for Sustainable Management of Forests" was adopted at the United Nations Conference on Environment and Development (UNCED). This statement presented principles for various methods of sustainable management of forests; however, it was not a treaty.

Of special note is the fact that the equatorial countries' national policies, regional development, urbanization, and wood exportation greatly influence tropical forests. Forest destruction is also closely related to other factors such as the above-mentioned long-range transboundary air pollution that causes acid rain, and sulfur and nitrogen oxide control. Therefore, deforestation cannot be solved unless these other issues are also taken into consideration. Incidentally, the International Tropical Timber Organization (ITTO) is one of the institutes that are deeply involved in tropical forest management.

3.5. *Events related to wild animals*

1971: In order to preserve valuable wetlands, 77 countries adopted the "Convention on Wetlands of International Importance, Especially as Waterfowl Habitat" in Ramsar, Iran.

1973: Given that an international treaty was absolutely necessary for protection of wild animals, particularly the rare species, 120 countries including Japan signed the Convention on International Trade in Endangered Species of Wild Fauna and Flora, in Washington, D.C., America.

1992: At the Earth Summit, 163 nations including Japan signed the Convention on Biological Diversity, for preservation of the diversity of wildlife, not only in eco-systems and in species, but also at the level of genes. It came into force in 1994. Some issues remain unresolved such as those of regulations for the use of genetic resources, and of technology transfer in biotechnology.

2008: COP9 for the Convention on Biological Diversity was held in Bonn, Germany. Among other topics, the 2010 target of lowering the rate of biodiversity loss was discussed.

4. Global Warming Regulations

At the Kyoto Conference on Prevention of Global Warming held from December 1–10 in 1997, a standard proposal for the reduction target of CO_2 emissions was submitted by each country. According to this proposal, reduction targets of 0% by the US, 2.5% by Japan, and 15% by the EU were submitted, respectively. Since the differences were so remarkable, Chairperson Estrada began to negotiate with each country. As a result, while Japan did not change its initial proposal, the US changed its reduction target from 0% to 5% and the EU from 15% to 10% on December 5.

On December 8, while Japan yielded from 2.5% to 4%, the US backpedalled from 5% to 2% and so did the EU from 10% to 8%. At this stage, US Vice President Gore revealed his flexibility and Chairperson Estrada himself proposed Japan 4.5%, US 5%, and EU 6%, respectively, one day before the final agreement. On December 10, the COP3 final reduction targets were determined.

Agreement over the reduction targets was barely achieved at COP3, and it left many issues unresolved. COP4 was held in Buenos Aires in 1998, and COP5 in Bonn in 1999, to discuss additional issues. However, rifts resurfaced between the US, EU and Japan at COP6 held in The Hague in November 2000. On March 28, 2001, after the Bush administration came into office, the US declared its intention to leave the Kyoto Protocol.

Reportedly, the main reason for this decision was that the Bush administration, in valuing the energy industry's support, decided that the US's target of a 7% reduction was more detrimental to the American economy than beneficial. Moreover, the US criticized the Kyoto Protocol as unfair in that developing countries were not subject to it.

An unofficial ministerial meeting was held in New York on April 21, in an attempt to persuade the US to reach an international agreement based on the Kyoto Protocol. The US, however, rejected the Protocol, and stated that it would propose an alternative international framework at COP6 that was to be resumed in July 2001 in Bonn, Germany.

It was left undecided whether the Protocol should enter into force without the US's ratification. The US was not the only cause of dissent, however; there was discord between the EU and Japan too. While Japan insisted on leaving emissions trading to the discretion of each nation, taking forest sinks into full consideration, the EU continued to assert that emissions trading must be regulated, without taking much notice of forest sinks. Meanwhile, developing countries advocated further support for technological transfer.

Conferences of the Parties to the United Nations Framework Convention on Climate Change still take place every year. In addition, since COP11 in 2005 when the first Meeting of the Parties to the Kyoto Protocol (MOP) took place, COP and MOP have been held together annually.

More than 10,000 delegates from 180 countries gathered together for COP13 in 2007. On December 3, 2007, Australia, which had been refusing to officially endorse the Kyoto Protocol, finally signed and ratified the Protocol. Thus, the US became the only developed country that had not yet ratified the Protocol.

COP14 took place in Poznań, Poland, in December 2008. Dr. Rajendra K. Pachauri, Chairperson of the IPCC, emphasized in his address the importance of political leadership in combating global warming. He also indicated his intention to propose to the

UN Secretary-General that future COPs should be held at summit-level by the world leaders, including the President-Elect of the US.

COP15, held in Copenhagen in 2009, ended with the Copenhagen Accord; it was agreed that measures should be taken to keep rises in temperature below 2 degrees Celsius, in response to the IPCC reports.

5. Corporate Responsibility for Global Environmental Issues

It is clear that environmental issues today have become grave, global matters, not merely local pollution incidents. It goes without saying that corporations need to comply with the Basic Environment Law and the Environment Impact Assessment Law, enacted respectively in 1993 and 1997. Companies should make systematic and proactive efforts to achieve the goal of "zero emissions," so that their social responsibilities can be fulfilled.

Of special importance are the following: (1) reducing environmental impacts, (2) achieving "zero emissions" and thorough recycling of resources, and (3) reforming accounting standards for environmental budgets.

5.1. *Reducing environmental impacts*

In the case of the US, as a measure of reducing environmental impacts, the so-called Muskie Act was enacted in 1970 to regulate automobile emissions. In 1980, the Comprehensive Environmental Response, Compensation, and Liability Act (commonly known as the Superfund) was enacted for disposal of toxic waste, and in 1990 the then President Bush signed the Clean Air Act Amendments, which may lead to the passage of a Zero-Emissions Vehicle Act.

In order to quantify environmental impacts, it is necessary to classify and define environmental costs. According to the United States Environmental Protection Agency (EPA), environmental costs are divided into Direct Costs, Hidden Costs, Contingent Costs (penalties, fines, future liabilities), and Less Tangible Costs. Lowering or eliminating these costs leads to reduction of environmental impacts.

Furthermore, in order to reduce environmental impacts, all environmental loads involved in the entire lifecycle of products and their packages must be minimized. This includes environmental loads in procurement of raw materials, production, distribution, sales, consumption, and disposal. We need to develop a process that reduces the amounts of solid, liquid and gas wastes that are released into the atmosphere, underground, and into the sea, minimizes pollutants, and releases eco-friendly substances instead.

5.2. *Achieving "zero emissions" and thorough recycling of resources*

To meet such needs, many companies are engaged in efforts to achieve zero emissions and a thorough recycling system.

For example, Fuji Xerox has adopted a scheme of inverse manufacturing, whereby re-use and recycling are taken into consideration at the level of product development. As many as 130 design requirements such as ease of dismantling, use of common parts, and selection of materials are listed in the "Recycle-Oriented Product Design Guidelines," drawn up by its engineers. The company's subsidiaries and subcontractors are also given "Guidelines on Procurement for Recycling" to ensure that the recycling-oriented production system is strictly adhered to, as well as "Guidelines on Green Procurement" to reduce the amount of potentially damaging chemical substances in their products.

Nissan Motor, on the other hand, has developed various clean technologies in order to create zero-emission vehicles. Nissan Sentra CA is a fruit of these technologies; it received an award for its clean technologies from the California Environmental Protection Agency — the only gasoline-fueled car to qualify as a Zero-Emissions Vehicle.

These clean technologies were further developed for Nissan Bluebird Sylphy, a mass-produced car model for the domestic market, which qualified as an ultralow-emissions vehicle (ULEV) in Japan, with more than 50% emissions reduction. Its fuel efficiency has been further improved, and it met the 2010 fuel-efficiency target level.

Meanwhile, Chubu Electric Power is endeavoring to establish a reactor fuel cycle by re-using uranium and plutonium obtained from used fuel. If this technology is established, it will be possible to generate energy that is usable for over 1,000 years.

5.3. *Reforming accounting standards for environmental budgets*

The Financial Accounting Standards Board (FASB) sets down the following accounting standards for environmental issues:

- SFAS 5: Accounting for Contingencies: accounting methods for contingencies, which take probability and degree of estimableness into consideration.
- SFAS Interpretation 14: disclosure of the minimum amount in cases where reasonable estimation of the amount of a loss is not possible.

By the Emerging Issues Task Force (EITF):

- 89–13: Accounting for the Cost of Asbestos Removal (related to the Asbestos Material Ban on manufacture, importation, processing, and distribution of asbestos-containing products that the US Environmental Protection Agency issued in 1989, effective until 1993, based on the 1976 Toxic Substances Control Act).
- 90–8: Capitalization of Costs to Treat Environmental Contamination.
- 93–5: Accounting for Environmental Liabilities.

By the American Institute of Certified Public Accountants (AICPA):

- 96–1: Environmental Remediation Liabilities.

As for Regulation S-X, the US Securities and Exchange Commission (SEC) demands disclosure of total potential environmental costs, and analysis and disclosure of serious effects, serious concerns, disputes, and undecided matters of administrative accountability, and anticipated trends and events in relation to environmental laws such as Clean Air Act, Clean Water Act, Resource Conservation and Recovery Act, and Superfund Act.

In assessing corporate activities and accomplishments in terms of social and psychological risk, pollution risk, economic risk, and benefits ascribable to financial institutions, investors and consumers, what is crucial is quantitative financial analysis — in particular, cost-performance analysis and cost-effectiveness analysis. As a reference, Table 3 reproduces part of IBM Japan's financial statements related to environmental issues.

The more solid accounting standards are, the more easily account statements of corporations, industries and even nations can be compared, which will enhance reliability. In that sense, if we are to have healthy environmental accounting, we must first establish accounting standards that are widely acceptable on a global scale. If these standards prompt disclosure of environmental activities, they will help companies improve their environmental information assessment systems, while benefiting investors and users in environmental investment management. Thus, the society as a whole will be enriched and the quality of life enhanced.

The Japan Environment Agency (now the Ministry of Environment) published "A Draft Guideline for Measuring and Announcing Environmental Costs" in March 1999. According to this guideline, the costs of environmental conservation are classified as follows:

(1) Direct costs for reducing environmental impacts;
(2) Indirect costs for reducing environmental impacts;
(3) Costs for reducing environmental impacts involved in the usage and disposal of manufactured and distributed products;
(4) Research and development costs for reducing environmental impacts;
(5) Social costs for reducing environmental impacts;
(6) Other costs related to environmental conservation.

Table 3:   IBM Japan's 1997 Financial Statements (in million dollars)

Environmental Costs

— Environmental management and human resources	34.4	(41.3)
— Environmental consultants	2.4	(2.9)
— Environmental research	3.6	(4.3)
— Permits and licenses	0.9	(1.1)
— Waste disposal	15.9	(19.1)
— Water quality control and wastewater disposal	19.1	(22.9)
— Atmospheric emission management	3.1	(3.7)
— Groundwater monitoring and management	0.9	(1.1)
— Environmental management system maintenance	1.1	(1.3)
— Waste and raw material recycling	3.7	(4.4)
— Superfund facilities and old office maintenance	7.0	(8.4)
— Other environmental management	3.0	(3.6)
Total	95.1	(114.1)

Estimated Environmental Savings and Cost Avoidance

— Pollution prevention activities	27.6	(33.1)
— Facilities recycling	13.1	(15.7)
— Reform and reduction of packaging materials	29.8	(35.8)
— Energy-saving effects	27.0	(32.4)
— Forward-planning of superfund facilities and office maintenance	10.4	(12.5)
— Insurance savings	9.1	(10.9)
— Avoidance of leak repair costs	25.0	(30.0)
— Avoidance of legal compliance costs	53.5	(64.2)
Total	195.5	(234.6)

Source: *The Nikkei*, June 4, 1999.
Note: Numbers in parentheses are 1999 figures.

While costs are comparatively measurable, in general, it is not easy to measure benefits, effectiveness, and contribution. Commonly used concepts include savings effects, reduction effects, and opportunity costs such as cost avoidance. Even with such concepts, however, direct effects may be measured, but indirect effects or ripple effects are likely to be overlooked.

6. Conclusion

In this chapter, we first discussed environmental risks such as pollution problems, and then examined crisis management regulations for global environmental issues of global warming, ozone depletion, acid rain, forest destruction, and loss of biodiversity. Following that, we reviewed the recent situation of global warming regulations, speculating briefly on the future trends, and discussed the difficulties involved in negotiating international treaties. Then, in relation to corporate responsibility in environmental issues, we focused on the three topics of reducing environmental impacts, achieving zero emissions and a thorough recycling system, and improving accounting standards for solving environmental issues.

Now that environmental issues have spread worldwide, crisis management needs to be on a global, macro level; yet, it must be meticulously attended to on a local, micro level too. It is hoped that crisis management for environmental issues is managed on both levels harmoniously, and that a good environmental protection system will be constructed to sustain the growth and welfare of individuals, companies, nations, and the world as a whole.

References

Brown, Lester, *Ecology: How Environmental Trends are Reshaping the Global Economy*, Tachibana Shuppan, 1998.

Chiba, Mikio, *Toyota Environmental Management*, Kanki Shuppan, 2001.

Iguma, Hitoshi, *Environmental Bankruptcy: Environmental Corporate Selection Has Begun*, Nikkan Kogyo Shinbunsha, 1999.

Ishikawa, Akira and Hiroshi Furuta, "Information Systems for Environmental Accounting," *Kankyo Shinbunsha* (*Environment Newspaper*), 2000.

Ishizaki, Chuji *et al.* (eds.), *Crisis Management and Accounting Information*, Gakubunsha, 1997.

Itokawa, Hideo, *Would the Human Race Be Annihilated in the 21st Century!?*, Tokuma Shoten, 1994.

Nemoto, Kazuyasu, *An Introduction to Environmental Risk Management*, Hakuto Shobo, 1999.

Nishizawa, Junichi *et al.*, *Humankind Will Become Extinct in the Next Eighty Years*, Toyo Keizai Shinpo, 2000.

Chapter 9

Business Intelligence and Knowledge Management*

1. Intellectual Capital: Definitions and Modeling Approaches

1.1. Assessing "invisible assets" objectively

I have studied "knowledge" and "knowledge management" in more than 20 different disciplines over the past 40 years. The equivalent of "knowledge" in Japanese is "*chishiki*" (knowledge), "*rikai*" (understanding), or "*tsugyo*" (mastery). These words are generally used in terms of individuals gradually gaining knowledge and making it their own (knowledge, understanding, and then mastery). Knowledge management, on the other hand, is a study that aims to realize and make use of the value of knowledge in terms of organizational profits and social welfare. Knowledge science and knowledge engineering, disciplines of wider scopes, form the foundation of knowledge management.

The 21st century is said to be the era of "Knowledge Creation"; the world has moved on from competing for visible resources and assets to competing for invisible knowledge. Consequently, the discipline of knowledge management, which has traditionally been science- and engineering-based, has broadened further to include social science, humanities, and medicine. Incidentally, in my attempt to

---

*This chapter is a revised version of the article in *Aoyama Management Review*, No. 3, April 2003, pp. 24–33.

promote knowledge management in an even wider sense, not just as a school of thought, I have suggested an Intellectual Olympics.

In the book titled *Knowledge Management Activities and International Management* (Zeimu Keiri Kyokai — Tax and Accounting Association, 2002), I examined the meaning and definitions of "knowledge" from nine different perspectives. They are as follows:

- Value-Added Knowledge Theory
- Knowledge Theory in Information Science
- Intellectual Capital Theory
- Value Creation-Oriented Knowledge Theory
- Formalism Approach to Knowledge
- Organizational Knowledge Theory
- Explicit and Implicit Knowledge Theory
- Knowledge Study Theory
- Purposive Knowledge Theory.

In this chapter, the meaning and contents of intellectual capital theory, intangible asset theory, and human capital theory will be examined, with particular emphasis on their major schools of thought and the conditions for success in human resource management. In doing so, it will be shown that intellectual capital management theory, intellectual financial management theory, and intangible capital management theory can be considered as sub-disciplines of knowledge management, or as specialized studies of the value of knowledge and property rights.

In terms of quantification, disclosure, and management, the ranges are clearer in knowledge management than in intellectual capital (IC) management, as the latter deals with broader and newer areas of knowledge. This means that IC management has more potential for transcending the conceptual or linguistic limits. Particularly in the area of intellectual property rights, quantitative and non-quantitative descriptions have to be precise, in order to avoid legal ambiguity.

In this chapter, the terminology of intellectual capital and its position in corporate management will be explored first. We will also discuss the connotation of capital in economics and how to understand intellectual capital in accounting and finance theory and balance sheet theory.

1.2. *Modern economics has disregarded intellectual capital*

In the book *Knowledge Management Activities and International Management* (2002), I defined knowledge in terms of intellectual capital theory as "the basic driving force that generates intellectual capital." In general, intellectual capital generated by intellectual activities is invisible capital, as opposed to visible capital. In 1995, Skandia Ltd., a Swedish insurance company, listed invisible assets for the first time under the heading "Intellectual Capital" in the appendix of its financial statements. Since then, the term has come to be widely used almost interchangeably with the accounting terms, "Intangible Assets" or "Intellectual Assets."

Hudson (1993), however, notes that it is the economist John Kenneth Galbraith who first used the term "Intellectual Capital" in his letter to the Polish economist Michal Kalecki in 1969. In this letter, Galbraith writes that there is no knowing just how much the world is indebted to Kalecki for the intellectual capital he has provided the world with over the last several decades.

According to *Yuhikaku Economics Dictionary*, within modern economics, land and labor tend to be considered as the original factors of production, while visible, tangible things such as production facilities (factories, machines, etc.), inventory and houses are called assets. Invisible fruits of intellect, however, are usually not covered in modern economics. For instance, Marxian economics defines capital as "self-expanding value." Such an abstract definition does not include intellectual capital, e.g., copyrights.

As for "capital" in accounting, capital in a broad sense refers to liabilities and equity, i.e., total capital. In this sense, capital means "net assets," which consist of equity capital and earnings. Note, however, that this definition focuses on sources of capital only, and again there is no mention of the use of capital or other sources of capital that should be assessed.

Here, we should note that from the perspective of corporate accounting, or more precisely, corporate financial reporting, capital accounts belong to credit accounts, whereas asset accounts belong to debit accounts; that is, there is a fundamental difference between the two ("cause and effect" or "supplier and supplied"). In terms of knowledge, it is possible to distinguish between "intellectual capital" ("supplier": knowledge-related intellectual activities), and "intellectual assets" ("supplied": the resulting re-useable knowledge). In this chapter, however, we will not make such a fine distinction between the two. We could also say that it is fundamentally flawed to attempt to account for all capital and assets using the two-dimensional, dualistic (cause and effect, income and expense) double-entry bookkeeping system, as it ignores the dynamic in-between space.

If we are to add invisible assets on top of such a framework, the conceptual framework itself might collapse. Thus, we need to redesign the traditional accounting system into a multi-dimensional system, to accommodate the slippery element of "intellectual capital." In the next section, the case of Skandia will be further examined and three major modeling approaches are introduced.

2. Intellectual Capital as Corporate Value

2.1. *Skandia's classification method*

There are many ways to categorize intellectual capital (assets). Skandia, the company commonly said to have played a major role in defining intellectual capital, has its own classification system, namely categorization of assets as sources that generate value. It has been cited many times in various books.

Whereas intangible assets have already gained recognition to a certain degree, other intellectual assets that have not yet made it onto the balance sheet can be categorized as "off-balance sheet intellectual assets." The key is how to categorize these off-balance sheet intellectual assets and translate them into assets that generate value.

Skandia divides off-balance sheet intellectual capital into "human capital" and "structural capital" ("human" vs. "artificial," or "structural" vs. "non-structural"); the latter is then divided into "customer capital" and "organized capital" ("external" vs. "internal"). Then, "organized capital" is further divided into "process capital" and "innovation capital" ("process revision and improvement" vs. "non-process revision," such as intellectual property rights and OBS intellectual assets). Thus, a neat tree structure is formed.

Based on the following four hypotheses, namely that human capital is closely related to customer capital (H1), that human capital has a strong connection with structural capital (H2), that customer capital is closely linked to structural capital (H3), and that structural capital is closely tied to corporate performance (H4), Bontis, Keow, and Richardson (2000) come to the following conclusions:

(1) Human capital is as important as material capital, no matter what industry the business is in.
(2) Human capital has more influence on the structure of non-service industries than service industries.
(3) Customer capital, in whatever line of business, has a big impact on structural capital.
(4) Regardless of whatever the business is, development of structural capital is positively correlated with corporate performance.

2.2. *Biased facts and information in financial statements*

According to the Value Dynamics Framework started by a group in MIT, intellectual assets are divided into those accumulated by experience, those generated by perceived value in markets (mainly by customers), by formal elements, and by regulatory elements. There is a considerable emphasis on the psychological and cognitive aspects. From the viewpoint of the place, environment, or specific situation where intellectual assets exist, they can be divided into those that derive from markets, organizations, systems, culture, products, and specific individuals.

In 1996, 43 Swiss companies had already included intellectual assets in the appendices of their financial statements, but no company

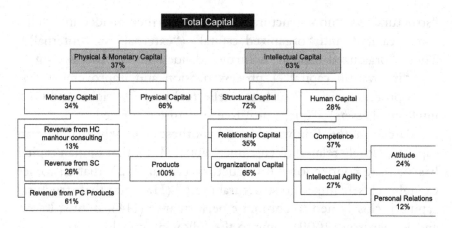

Figure 5:   Classification of Assets by Skandia

Source: Distinction Tree, Supplement to The Annual Report 1997, Skandia Intelligent Enterprising.

in North America had done so yet. As an example of this tendency among European companies, in the appendix of Skandia's 1997 financial statement, which divides total capital into "intellectual capital" and "physical and monetary capital," the former is a staggering 63%, whereas the latter is only 37% (see Figure 5).

Thus, if the above represents the reality of capital accounts, it follows that the prevalent practice of financial statements does not offer a faithful report of capital accounts, and it does not reflect reality. In other words, even though the world has already moved on to a new era of Knowledge Society, Knowledge Capitalism, and Knowledge Businesses, the form and content of financial reporting has not changed much from the previous era of Manufacturing Society, Industrial Capitalism, and Tangible Product Businesses.

According to a survey of Fortune 500 companies and 300 companies in Canada, while 76% of the companies recognized the importance of corporate ethics and corporate culture, only 37% of these companies attempted to assess those assets. Similarly, despite the fact that 76% pointed out the importance of core competencies, only 36% had begun to evaluate their own core competencies. Incidentally, core competencies have the highest figure (37%) among human capital in Skandia's 1997 financial report.

Of course, in dealing with intellectual capital, we must deal with its legal side; intellectual property rights and intangible property rights must be taken into account and categorized. Generally speaking, it seems reasonable to classify these rights into three broad categories of industrial property rights, copyrights, and business method patents. Industrial property rights can be further divided into rights for intellectual creation, or business signifiers such as trademarks and brands, and others.

On the other hand, copyrights, which the Internet has made even more complex, contain diverse categories such as those for presentation, exhibition, copying, and translation. Figure 6 presents a list of intellectual property rights according to this classification system.

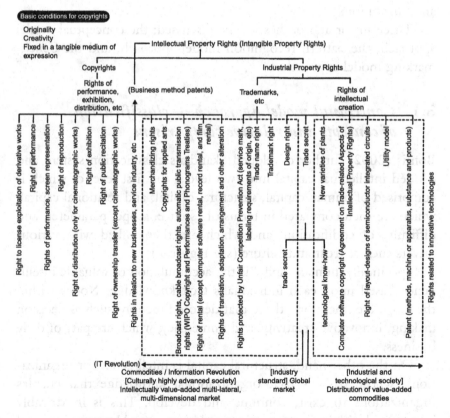

Figure 6: The Concepts of Intellectual Property Rights

Source: Adapted from Moriya Uchida, *How to Visualize and Use Intellectual Capital* (Nikkan Kogyo Shinbunsha, 2001, p. 184).

Next, we will explore the different kinds of modeling approaches for intellectual capital management.

3. Modeling Approaches for Establishing Intellectual Capital

In this section, we examine several major modeling approaches for establishing intellectual capital and for successful IC management. "Modeling approach" herein refers to methods for clarifying companies' intellectual capital, translating it into new products and services that are based on corporate purposes and objectives, establishing new core competencies, and creating new infrastructures for organizations and innovations.

Three major approaches will be discussed: the conceptual model approach, the pattern recognition model approach, and the benchmarking model approach.

3.1. *Conceptual model approach — classification of concepts and relative comparisons*

Bontis (2002) further developed Skandia's classification system and divided intellectual capital into two levels; the first level of which is comprised of human capital, structural capital, and relational capital, which are each compared in terms of essence, scope, parameter, and difficulty of codification, and which are then linked with various drivers such as trust and culture (see Figure 7).

Specifically, human capital is the accumulation of valuable intelligence based upon each individual's tacit knowledge. Nodes within the scope are, therefore, those that denote functions such as decision making, innovative creativity, and immediacy, which are part of daily business.

On the other hand, structural capital is intelligence for organizations, whose basis is tacit organizational knowledge that enables organizations to exist, continue and develop. This is inextricably intertwined with intensive routines and is supported by organizational culture.

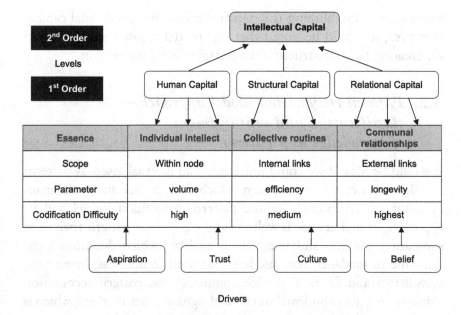

Figure 7: Conceptual Model of Intellectual Capital
Source: Adapted from Bontis (2002, p. 31).

Relational capital is regarded as the accumulation of intelligence with respect to external organizations, including national and local governments. It refers to potential capital in the relations between the company and those other organizations.

As for the essential differences between parameter and difficulty of codification, while we tend to focus on the quantity and quality of parameters, with human capital, we are more likely to focus on the degree of difficulty of codification. In contrast, the required parameters for structural capital are effectiveness and efficiency, and its degree of codification difficulty is medium. With regard to relational capital, parameters are evolution-oriented, while the codification difficulty is assessed to be the highest.

This kind of conceptual model can be considered as a development of Skandia's intellectual capital classification system. Skandia's model was a mere tree structure chart, and the criteria for evaluation were unclear; this model has clearer criteria, and its drivers are of universal nature. Therefore, we can say that with this model, we are one step closer to establishing the standard model for intellectual capital. However, it should be noted that this model is just a starting point for creating the infrastructure for organizational innovation.

3.2. *Pattern recognition model approach —* *classification and management* *of knowledge as a pattern*

It would be ideal if we could understand intellectual assets as patterns and develop a classification system which enables their successful management. As an example of the pattern recognition model and its approach, its military use is well-known; e.g., sound pattern analysis of submarine engines, and image map analysis, which determines the outcome of guidance systems. It is also used in business; investment consultants and financial service companies use pattern recognition software to detect abnormal trends and signs in stock markets, which is a good example of civil application of the military modeling approach.

The application of this pattern recognition model approach to anomaly detection is not limited to accounting and finance. Other examples include quality control in manufacturing, use of electrocardiograms in medical care, reconstruction of original bodies from bone structure in forensics, fingerprint/voice-print access control systems, measurement of students' understanding according to patterns in their academic results, document management by character recognition, detailed classification of products, pattern recognition for ATMs and ticket machines, etc. In this sense, there is room for an even wider use of pattern recognition in knowledge management and IC management.

To promote this, Davis (2002) develops a relationship diagram shown in Figure 8, as the core taxonomy of knowledge patterns. This knowledge meta-pattern array contains, quite naturally, reputational capital including images, brands, and reputation, which need to be cultivated, developed and maintained as the core of IC management/ scorecard companies, as well as intellectual assets and intellectual property rights.

In total, there are 33 items in this core taxonomy; since they are patterns, they are shown with respect to their relations to each other,

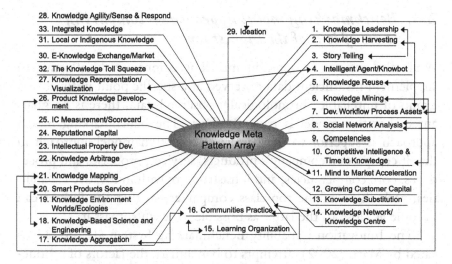

Figure 8:   Diagram of Pattern Recognition Models

Source: Adapted from Davis (2002).

rather than independently. While the comparative importance of each item is divided into three segments in the cobweb chart, this is only for convenience and is subject to change, depending on the scale and combinations of the relationships. It is also clearly stated that the number of items shown is not definite as this chart is not conclusive yet.

As there is not enough space to explain each item, I will highlight only the most important items:

(1) Knowledge Leadership
(2) Mind to Market Acceleration (enthusiasm, perseverance and intellectual methods that turn concepts into products and services)
(3) Knowledge Mapping (methods for improving the quality of knowledge performance).

Successful Knowledge Mapping, in particular, is key to successful knowledge management and IC management. Just as human genome mapping has been crucial for the Human Genome Project, if we can map organizational knowledge perfectly in whatever way, it will likely prove to be an invaluable asset for the organization.

3.3. Benchmarking model approach — comparing to see if it is of the highest level

While the pattern recognition model is comparatively effective to supplement insufficient data observed at a specific point in time, or a group of unreliable chronologically observed data, there is no guarantee that this model is truly the best. The benchmarking model approach is superior to the pattern recognition model approach in that it compares a company's products, services, processes and procedures, core competencies, and infrastructure with innovative capabilities, with those of the top-class companies, so that the former can become as close to the latter as possible, or even surpass it.

The Innovation Capability Benchmarking System (ICBS), advocated by Marti (2002), attempts to benchmark the factors of production and know-how of top-class innovative companies in the global market. The eight key factors covered here are: emerging new requirements, project objectives, new products and services, new processes and procedures, new core competencies, new professional core competencies, organizational innovation, and organizational infrastructure for financial performance.

The premise of the ICBS is that competition does not lie in products and services themselves, but in potential and existing competencies that make them possible; its aim is to detect such competencies. More precisely, true competition lies in a company's future competencies that will bring about new systems, products and services, against world-class companies' future core competencies.

These competencies can be divided into the innovative ability that enables new systems and procedures derived from insightful projects, and the ability to evaluate innovative infrastructure that supports new pending projects. Of course, a proper assessment model for the present system and procedures is vital too; this has to be continually developed.

In order to develop assessment systems, a global assessment diagram for innovative capabilities has been designed, with an innovation capabilities balance sheet. Part of the balance sheet is shown in Figure 9.

M & L	Project	New Fashion Products Development and Production
	Competitor	Zara

ASSETS	LIABILITIES	
1. NEW PRODUCTS	**1. NEW PRODUCTS**	
1.2 Price/	1.1 Design	
Quality relationship	1.3 Embodied service	
1.7 Conformance	1.4 New trends adaptation	
1.8 Garment selection	1.5 Fabric quality	
	1.6 Fashion	
2. NEW PROCESSES		
2.1 Customer needs	**2. NEW PROCESSES**	
identification	2.2 Discovering emerging needs	
2.5 Design CAD	2.3 Selecting market segment	
2.6 Manufacturing CAM	2.4 Creativity	
	2.7 Supply chain architecture	
3. NEW CORE CAPABILITIES	2.8 Process architecture	
3.2 Supply chain	2.9 Logistics	
architecture		
	3. NEW CORE CAPABILITIES	Consolidated
5. INNOVATION	3.1 Fashion creation	Reliability
INFRASTRUCTURE	3.3 Design for	Index
5.2 R&D integration	manufacturability DFM	xx%
	3.4 Supply chain design	
	3.5 3D concurrent engineering	
	3.6 Quick development and production	
	5. INNOVATION INFRASTRUCTURE	
	5.1 Innovation and strategy	
	5.3 Technology standard	
	5.4 R&D organization	
	5.5 Innovation resource allocation	
	5.6 Technology information systems	
	5.7 Technology management systems	

Figure 9: Innovation Capabilities Balance Sheet

Source: Adapted from Marti (2002).

Upon closer examination of the items in the balance sheet, we notice that there is a heavy emphasis on processes and systems. We will not discuss it in detail in this chapter, except to say that this balance sheet is different from the IC balance sheet developed by Telia, which is based more on human resources (Seetharaman *et al.*, 2002).

This balance sheet includes recruitment capital, and education and training capital in assets and liabilities accounts. Moreover, personnel turnover rate, education and training costs, sick leave costs and social activity costs are included in the profit and loss statement.

As a tool for assessing B/S and I/S, indices such as Knowledge Capital Value and Overhead-to-Asset Conversion Efficiency (OTAE) have been developed. This modeling approach can be said to represent a more traditional management analysis model, different from the benchmarking model approach.

4. Valid Assessment of Intellectual Capital Management

In this chapter, starting with knowledge and modern economics, we have explored IC management through understanding the concepts of knowledge management and IC management, and their comparative analysis.

For that purpose, we have tried to grasp the meaning of IC and to classify it, and we briefly examined major IC modeling approaches, such as conceptual modeling, pattern recognition modeling, and benchmarking modeling approaches. As these are not the only approaches, we briefly touched on more traditional management analysis modeling approaches as well.

With these approaches, and as other new ones emerge, knowledge management and IC management will continue to develop further. For example, Skandia independently developed the dolphin navigator system — an IT tool which gives access to everyone in a group. Because of this, Skandia's navigator system is used to exchange experiences and knowledge among group members, not just as a reporting tool. This system is therefore considered to be a driver that enhances intellectual capital.

It is hoped that IC management will be developed wisely and continually, not just as a decisive tool for maintaining competitive advantage, but as a tool for achieving social responsibility, developed in response to powerful concepts and ideas, and making full use of effective intellectual drivers and business intelligence.

References

Bontis, Nick (ed.), *World Congress on Intellectual Capital Readings*, Boston: Butterworth Heinemann, pp. 13–56 (2002).

Bontis, Nick, "Managing Organizational Knowledge by Diagnosing Intellectual Capital: Framing and Advancing the State of the Field," *International Journal of Technology Management*, Vol. 18, No. 5/6/7/8, pp. 433–462 (1999).

Bontis, Nick, W. C. Chong Keow, and Stanley Richardson, "Intellectual Capital and Business Performance in Malaysian Industries," *Journal of Intellectual Capital*, Vol. 1, No. 1, pp. 85–94 (2000).

Davis, Bryan, "The Power of Knowledge-Pattern Recognition" in *World Congress on Intellectual Capital Readings*, Nick Bontis (ed.), Boston: Butterworth-Heinemann, pp. 72–93 (2002).

Hudson, William J., *Intellectual Capital: How to Build It, Enhance It, Use It*, New York: John Wiley & Sons, p. 15 (1993).

Ishikawa, Akira (with Hiroshi Mieno), "An Expert System for Facial Restoration" in *Approximate Reasoning in Expert Systems*, M. M. Gupta *et al.* (eds.), Amsterdam: North-Holland, pp. 655–699 (1985).

Ishikawa, Akira, "The International Mathematical Olympiad," a keynote address given at the 13th International Conference on Systems Research and Cybernetics, Germany, July 30–August 4 (2001).

Ishikawa, Akira *et al.* (eds.), *Knowledge Management Activities and International Management*, Zeimu Keiri Kyokai, pp. 4–8 (2002).

Ishikawa, Akira, "A Framework for The Intellectual Olympics," *The Aoyama Journal of International Politics, Economics and Business*, Vol. 43, pp. 163–170 (1998).

Ishikawa, Akira, "Intellectual Olympics and Ten Representative Issues to be Resolved," a keynote address at the 20th Anniversary, Graduate School of Business Administration, the University of Macau, November 5 (2001).

Ishikawa, Akira, "Intellectual Olympics: Harnessing Human Intelligence for Worthwhile Applications," a keynote address presented at Executive World SympoFair 2000, Singapore, September 1–3 (2000).

Ishikawa, Akira, "Regional Systems and Administrative Management Issues and Prospects," a keynote address given at the 23rd Annual Convention of the Japanese Society of Administrative Management, Hiroshima City, Japan, September 23 (2000).

Ishikawa, Akira, "Reinventing Evaluation Judgment Systems and The Intellectual Olympics," a keynote address delivered at the 3rd International Symposium on a Culture of Peace and the Dialogue of Civilizations for the 3rd Millennium, Germany, August 2–7 (1999).

Ishikawa, Akira, "The Application of The Intellectual Olympics: Still Another Case," a paper presented at the Symposium on a Universal Theory Structure and Story Grammar Called The Hamiltonian, Germany, July 30 (2002).

Ishikawa, Akira, "The Intellectual Olympics," *The Bi-Monthly Journal of The BWW Society*, September/October, Vol. 2, No. 1, pp. 71–80. Also available at: http://www.bwwsociety.org/journal/html/intellolympics.htm.

Ishikawa, Akira, "The Prospectus of The Intellectual Olympics," invited presentation at the Fourth Annual Conference of the Knowledge Management Society of Japan, International Hall, Federation of Economic Organizations, Tokyo, Japan, February 3 (2001).

Ishikawa, Akira, "Theater Olympics: A Case of the Intellectual Olympics," a keynote address given at the 12th International Conference on Systems Research, Informatics and Cybernetics, Germany, July 31–August 5 (2000).

Kanamori, Hisao *et al.*, *Yuhikaku Economics Dictionary, 4th Edition*, Yuhikaku, p. 538 (2002).

Lynn, B. E., "Culture and Intellectual Capital Management: A Key Factor in Successful ICM Implementation," *International Journal of Technology Management*, Vol. 18, No. 5/6/7/8, p. 600 (1999).

Marti, Jose Maria Viedma, "Innovation Capability Benchmarking System (ICBS)" in *World Congress on Intellectual Capital Readings*, Nick Bontis (ed.), Boston: Butterworth-Heinemann, pp. 243–265 (2002).

Martin, William J., "Approaches to the Measurement of the Impact of Knowledge Management Programmes," *Journal of Information Sciences*, Vol. 26, No. 1, p. 25 (2000).

Okada, Eri, *Corporate Assessment and Intellectual Assets*, Zeimu Keiri Kyokai, pp. 74–75 (2002).

Seetharaman, A., Hadi Helmi Bin Zaini Sooria, and A. S. Saravanan, "Intellectual Capital Accounting and Reporting in the Knowledge Economy," *Journal of Intellectual Capital*, Vol. 3, No. 2, pp. 128–148 (2002).

Chapter 10

Business Intelligence
as Organizational Intelligence

1. Definition of Organizational Intelligence

In my previous books, I made a distinction between data, information, and intelligence (Ishikawa, 1986, 1988a, 1988b, 1993a, 1993b), based on ideas related to data processing, value addition, and decision making. In particular, I stated that if we classify decision-making into operational decision-making, managerial decision-making, and strategic decision-making, the corresponding types of information needed for each decision-making are, respectively, data, information, and intelligence. Therefore, according to this framework, strategic decision-making requires the highest quality of information, i.e., intelligence, especially business intelligence (BI) in the private sector.

The term "intelligence" thus connotes knowledge information, intelligently processed information, and, ideally, is equivalent to wisdom. Over the years, a new term has emerged: Organizational Intelligence. Matsuda (1994), an advocate of Organizational Intelligence, defines it as interaction, accumulation, and integration of human intelligence and machine intelligence that are inherent in any organization. He also divides organizational intelligence into processes and products. However, he does not explicitly state that organizational intelligence is derived from organizations, rather than individuals.

When we say organizational intelligence, we generally refer to intelligence generated by groups within an organization, rather than by organizations as a whole. Certainly, "group organization" cannot be ignored in the process of organizational intelligence production, and we should not disregard the fact that intelligence acquired by individuals has led to great inventions and discoveries in the past.

Another source of organizational intelligence is strategic partnerships or alliances. It should be noted that as people and companies become more closely linked through intricate networks, boundaries for organizational intelligence are increasingly blurred. In this current environment, knowledge is shared more frequently and to a greater extent than before. Also, it is possible that changes in organizational relationships (for example, from a loose alliance to M&A) would greatly influence the amount and quality of meta-organizational intelligence (intelligence generated by multiple organizations).

As will be discussed in this chapter, organizations have to design networks, make effective use of these networks, and continually improve them, in order to accumulate the necessary wisdom for generating organizational intelligence most effectively.

2. Production, Use, and Evaluation of Organizational Intelligence

Ishikawa *et al.* (1991) compare management issues in collecting, analyzing, and evaluating knowledge information, i.e., intelligence, with those on information. In the collection phase, one of the key issues is how to speedily collect or produce intelligence. It is the general assumption that the more processed or value-added information is, the closer it is to becoming useful intelligence. This is not always the case, however. Also, what is effective for individuals in creating intelligence does not always prove to be effective for organizations.

One good example is as follows: developing an expert system for financial analysis, which produced intelligence, led to a 40% reduction in a company's personnel cost, while the rate of return decreased by 60%. Why? Because while one department gained in productivity by implementing the expert system, which helped to cut down on the number of employees, in another department, where the redundant staff had been relocated and retrained, personnel cost increased more than the increase in sales. Therefore, the overall profit decreased more than in the previous period.

An effective and overall analysis of intelligence may help to resolve this dilemma. However, it is difficult to determine an appropriate time span for assessing this case; the downturn in the profit might prove temporary or long-term. Another important factor is the versatility of the developed software. If the software can be used in other departments as well, the cost reduction will be greater.

Another example of organizational intelligence involves a huge database of organic compounds for R&D called SPHINCS. Fujifilm Company, Japan, developed this database over many years and accumulated over 100,000 organic compounds. Surprisingly, from these organic compounds in the database, several thousand new compounds have been generated.

The original purpose of this database was to develop sensitized materials. However, a certain laboratory at Harvard University became interested in using this database for developing anti-cancer medicine. Thus far, a new reagent has been reported, whose efficacy in animal testing was over ten times more effective than previous ones.

There are two lessons to be drawn from these examples. Firstly, analysis and assessment are not independent of each other. Comprehensive analyses will inevitably include some form of evaluation. Cursory analyses, in contrast, are generally not of much use to management, unless the time span and know-how are clearly defined.

Secondly, the intelligence produced, used, and evaluated by an individual or a department is not always applicable in another department or throughout the entire organization. Therefore, organizational intelligence needs to be designed and developed on an organization-wide basis so that it can be utilized throughout the organization. If the expert system for financial analysis mentioned earlier could be used in all the departments of the organization, then they would all achieve the 40% reduction in personnel cost, which would make the total cost reduction a considerable sum. Companies with successful production, use, and evaluation of organizational intelligence include Microsoft, Intel, and Nintendo, among others.

3. Tools for Organizational Intelligence

The methods or techniques for producing organizational intelligence can be broadly divided into two kinds: the arts-oriented and the science-oriented. The former can also be viewed as a user-oriented approach, and the latter as a developer-oriented approach.

The former includes, for example, Value Chain Analysis and Critical Success Factor approach; its basic purpose is to find out what would help companies secure a competitive advantage against their competitors and end up victorious in a corporate war. The latter, on the other hand, includes tools such as Business Process Reengineering (BPR), Electronic Data Interchange (EDI), Groupware, RFID, and various BI suites and platforms. Its aim is to bring innovative concepts, solutions and standardization to organizations. To use a linguistic metaphor, the former is semantic, while the latter is syntactic.

Of course, this kind of dichotomy cannot cover every single technique and method. Since approaches for creating organizational intelligence are likely to be new and novel, and are related to creation and discovery, we have to look into these areas as well. Hence, if we assume that the ultimate goal of organizational intelligence is related to creativity, we have to examine as many creativity tools as possible.

Takahashi (1993) says that there are more than 300 kinds of creativity techniques, and he introduces 91 techniques. He classifies the creativity techniques into four categories: the divergent thinking methods such as Brainstorming and Checklist methods; the convergent thinking methods such as the KJ and PERT methods; combinations of these two methods such as Work Design Method; and the attitudinal methods which encompass Transactional Analysis and Creative Dramatics (Takahashi, 1993, pp. 253–255). He further states that while Brainstorming is one of the most well-known methods in the world, the KJ method and the NM method are most popular in Japan, while the Checklist and PERT methods are gaining in popularity. However, TRIZ — the innovative problem-solving method — is not included here. Goldfire Innovator, a TRIZ software, enables competitive analysis.

In the next section, more details of idea-generating or idea-creating methods will be explored that should facilitate the development and enhancement of GDSS, NSS, and Electronic Meeting System (EMS) (Ishikawa, 1968; Ishikawa *et al.*, 1981a, 1981b; Ishikawa and Mieno, 1992; Ishikawa and Hirota, 1994; Takahashi, 1993; and Nunamaker *et al.*, 1991).

4. Idea Generation Methods

Idea generation methods, based on the four categories mentioned above, will be further examined here, starting with the divergent thinking methods.

4.1. *Divergent idea generation methods*

The major methods in this school include Free Association, Forced Association, and Analogous Idea Association. Free Association Methods are further classified into Brainstorming (Parnes and Harding, 1962), Card BS (Takahashi, 1987), Brainwriting (Geschka and Schlicksuppe, 1971), and Electronic Brainstorming (Nunamaker *et al.*, 1991).

Card BS, Brainwriting, and Electronic Brainstorming are derivatives of Brainstorming, which is one of the most well-known creativity methods. Card BS uses cards in the process of Brainstorming to help participants to create as many ideas as possible, to think multilaterally, and to draw on each other's ideas. Brainwriting, on the other hand, is called the 6-3-5 method because six participants offer three ideas each in five minutes. One of the characteristics of this method is the silent ambience; silent, individual thinking is blended with group thinking. Electronic Brainstorming is a method of brainstorming made possible by computer technology; its originality lies not in the method itself but in the drastic new environment in which the method is used. With the new computer technologies, ideas can be generated in parallel within a given period of time, and reorganized online more effectively.

Forced Association Methods include Morphological Analysis (Allen, 1966), Checklist (R&D Guidebook Editorial Committee, 1973), Matrix (Takahashi, 1989a), Attributes Identification (Ueno, 1959),

Desirable Point Identification (Takahashi, 1984), and the Gordon Method (Whiting, 1958).

Fritz Zwicky, the creator of the Morphological Method, says he developed this method because people tend to be too hasty and caught up in preconceived notions when solving a problem. To avoid this, we must not give up on a problem until it is proved unsolvable. The Checklist and the Matrix methods are well-known in their general structures, and both are logic-oriented, whereas Attributes Identification, Desirable Point Identification, and the Gordon Method are more semantic-oriented in that ideas are forced to be expressed as verbs in terms of grammar, subjectivity, and state-variables.

Another group of the Divergent Methods is the Analogous Idea Association Methods, which include Synectics (Alexander, 1965), the NM Method (Nakayama, 1965), and Bionics. Synectics, developed by William J. J. Gordon, aims to generate new ideas by combining two different attributes or by differentiating similar attributes. The NM Method, developed by Masakazu Nakayama, is characterized by a six-step process, namely: (1) setting the issue, (2) setting keywords, (3) exploring analogies, (4) exploring backgrounds of the analogies, (5) coming up with ideas, and (6) discovering solutions.

Bionics, on the other hand, starts with the study of biological systems, constructs models to mimic them, and then ends with the design of relevant equipment and machines. This approach is generally considered to be the reverse of Cybernetics, developed by Norbert Wiener.

4.2. *Convergent idea generation methods*

The convergent thinking methods may be divided into spatial approaches and temporal approaches. The former includes the KJ (Kawakita, 1975), Kozane (Umesao, 1989), Cross (Takahashi, 1989b) and ISOP (Ishikawa and Hirota, 1994) methods, whereas the latter includes PERT (Mori, 1964), Business Design (Nakamura, 1979), Cause-and-Effect Diagram (Ishihara, 1965), and Relevance Tree Methods (Ayres, 1970).

The KJ Method is quite well-known in Japan, but not so much in other countries. This method, named after Jiro Kawakita, was developed primarily as an anthropological technique for summarizing fieldwork findings. Collected data is recorded on cards, and by gathering similar data cards, findings can be easily summarized. This method, however, has been expanded into a scientific and systematic approach to problem-solving in both private and public sectors. The Kozane, Cross, and ISOP methods may be considered as variations of the KJ method. In particular, similar to Electronic Brainstorming, ISOP can be viewed as a computerized KJ Method; the process is automated, allowing it to create more ideas within a given time, and is over ten times faster than the traditional KJ method.

The temporal methods place a bigger emphasis on logics and relationships. PERT, developed by the US Navy, is one of the by-products of the US-Soviet Space Race in the 1950s. It is prevalent in the areas of Operations Research and Management Sciences. On the other hand, Business Design, Cause-and-Effect Diagram, and Relevance Tree methods are less structured and more relation-oriented, avoiding rigid formality in a wide range of areas.

4.3. *Combination methods*

The ZK (Katagata and Tajima, 1978), Input-Output (Whiting, 1963) and Work Design (Nadler, 1969) methods use combinations of the divergent and convergent thinking. The characteristics of these techniques are that divergent thinking and convergent thinking are repeatedly used, and they encompass a variety of domains.

For example, the ZK Method, developed by Zenji Katagata, encompasses three levels of thinking: the cognitive world, the imaginary world, and the reality. In creativity development, the biggest emphasis is placed on the cognitive world in the idea generation phase, while the imaginary world and the reality are more important in the solution phase. This approach therefore requires both divergent and convergent thinking to ensure a smooth process.

It is well-known that the first Input-Output Method was developed by GE for the purpose of exploring new design ideas for an automatic system. At that time, this approach consisted of a formulaic repetition of divergent and convergent thinking with certain restrictions, with emphasis on the step-by-step process and evaluation. Now, it has become diversified, and more open and less formulaic.

The Work Design Method, on the other hand, was initially limited to the area of systems design. However, as the ideal or normative approach and the realistic or specific approach have become more valued within this method, it has started to use combinations of divergent and convergent thinking more than it did before.

4.4. *Attitudinal approaches*

Interactive Methods and Dramatic Methods fall into this genre. The former is further classified into Transactional Analysis (Berne, 1958), Encounter Group (Rogers, 1973), and Counseling (Rogers, 1987), whereas the latter includes Psychodrama Analysis (Anzieu, 1960), Role Playing, and Creative Dramatics (Siks, 1973).

The main distinction between the Interactive Methods and the Dramatic Methods lies in the setting in which a player conceives ideas. In the former, the setting is of a clinical nature and does not always involve scenarios and stories, whereas in the latter, scenarios and stories are prerequisites.

Transactional Analysis was developed on the basis of a traditional psychoanalytic theory. While Freud categorized ego into super-ego, ego and id, Berne, who developed this Transactional Analysis method, conceived the structure of ego as P (Parents), A (Adults), and C (Children). Upon identifying psychoanalytic attributes of each character, interaction between these three characters is structurally analyzed, so as to help foster the personal growth and self-realization which form the basis for idea generation.

Encounter Group, on the other hand, is not a training method but a fully open, informal meeting where two facilitators play an important role in encouraging coordination and self-expression among participants without taking leadership.

Counseling Methods, from diagnostic approaches to psychoanalytic ones, have been developed since the 1930s. Both directional counseling and non-directional counseling have been conducted in order to solve problems of individuals as well as groups.

In Psychodrama Analysis, participants are required to act sponta-neously so that they can realize their undiscovered self, which in turn is related to generating new ideas. The main feature of Role Playing is that it aims to bring participants from the realm of reality into that of imagination, so that interaction between them may generate new thoughts and ideas.

Finally, Creative Dramatics, as the name implies, is a technique where children are led to realize the importance of the creative pro-cess and the joy of creation, by making them create their own stories without borrowing from stories they know. This can also be applied to managers and employees.

Table 4 shows a summary of major idea generation methods and approaches, from the viewpoints of techniques, objects, entities, application stages, and scenes of application.

Table 4: A Summary of Idea-Creation (Generation) Approaches (Representative)

Classification		Divergent (Diffusing) Idea-Creation Methods					Convergent Idea-Creation Methods			Integrative Methods	Attitudinal Idea-Creation Methods	
Sub-Classification		Free Association Methods	Compulsory Association Methods	Analogous Methods	Spatial Methods	Series Comparison Meth.		ZK & Work Design Met	Interact Methods	Dramatic Methods		
Techniques (Methods)		Brainstorming / Card Brainstorming / Brain Writing / Electronic Brainstorm.	Morphological Analysis / Check List / Matrix / Attributes Identifica. / Desiring PTS. Identifi.	Gordon / Synedics / N.M. / Bionics / Equivalent Value Transf	K.J. / Kozane / Cross / ISOP	PERT / Business Design (BD) / Characteristics Factor / Relevance Tree		Z.K. / Input-Output / Work Design	Transactional Analysis / Encounter Group / Counseling	Psychological Drama / Role Playing / Creative Dramatics		
Objects	Management	o o				o				o o		
	Employees	o o o	o o	o o o o	o	o		o				
	All		o o o o		o	o o o	o o	o	o o o o	o		
Entities	Individual			o	o							
	Group	o o o o	o o			o o	o o o	o	o	o o o		
	Individual/Group		o o o o	o o o	o o		o	o	o o o			
APPL., STG.	Formulation		o o					o		o		
	Solution	o o	o	o o o o		o		o o		o		
	All Stages	o o o o	o		o o o o	o o o		o o o	o o o	o		
APPL., DOM.	R&D, eng.		o o o	o o o				o o				
	Sales, Clr.								o	o o		
	All Kinds	o o o o	o o o	o o	o o o o	o o o o		o	o o			

Source: Adapted from Takahashi (1993, pp. 258–259).

5. Future of Organizational Intelligence

Organizations should continually introduce and improve methods and techniques for organizational intelligence, so that they can create organizational intelligence and strategic intelligence. What is important here is how to create new ideas quickly by using these methods. It is also vital to keep searching for the correct direction in which improvements should be made. For that, it may be necessary to stock inventories of creativity techniques on a larger scale. Furthermore, we would need to explore combinations of these techniques for each issue, to discover the best combination for generating organizational intelligence. To this end, we must conduct various experiments constantly and systematically.

There are many paths that organizational intelligence can take. One direction is, as mentioned earlier, to discover the know-how of producing organizational intelligence speedily by one or a few techniques, and the best combination of techniques for a given realm of organizational intelligence.

Another direction is to explore questions such as what kind of external system environment may be best suited to generating organizational intelligence, and what sort of internal network environment would be the most desirable. Of particular importance is the question of the key environmental factors — those that trigger the generation of organizational intelligence, and those that ignite and inspire each individual so that organizational intelligence may be continually produced.

Yet another direction is to develop a system that can maintain the balance between competition and cooperation among individual members, or among sectors, for the most desirable synergy effects that would produce organizational intelligence. This requires psychological and motivational studies on the interaction of individuals, groups and organizations.

As shown in many successful cases, the importance of the illogical, the irrational, and the accidental cannot be ignored either, so as to best produce quality-oriented, sustainable organizational intelligence.

References

Alexander, Tom, "Synectics Inventing by the Madness Method," *Fortune*, August, 1965.

Allen, Myron S., *Psycho-Dynamic Synthesis: The Key to Total Mind Power* (US: Parker Publishing, 1966).

Anzieu, D., *Le Psychodrame Analytique chez L'enfant* (Tokyo: Maki Shoten, 1960).

Ayres, R. U., *Technological Forecasting and Long-Range Planning* (New York: McGraw-Hill Book Co., Inc., 1970).

Berne, Fric, *An Introduction to Life Game* (Tokyo: Kawade Shobou, 1958).

Geschka, H. and H. Schlicksuppe, "Techniken der Problemlosung," Rationalislerung, 22, Jg. 1971 and also Information (Battelle, Frankfurt, 1971).

Ishihara, Katsuyoshi, *Quality Control Text in the Working Place* (Tokyo: JUSE, 1965).

Ishikawa, Akira, "Urban Problems and Systems Engineering," paper presented at the 1st International Conference on System Sciences, Honolulu, Hawaii, January 29–31, 1968.

Ishikawa, Akira, *An Introduction to Strategic Information System* (Tokyo: Japan Economic Newspaper, 1986).

Ishikawa, Akira, *The 5th Generation Computer and Industrial Management* (Tokyo: Yuuhikaku, 1988a).

Ishikawa, Akira (ed.), *What are Business Expert Systems?* (Tokyo: Yuuhikaku, 1988b).

Ishikawa, Akira, "Information Systems," in Kiyoshi Yamazaki and Shirou Takeda (eds.), *Textbook Global Management* (Tokyo: Yuuhikaku, 1993a), pp. 218–233.

Ishikawa, Akira, *Strategic Budgeting* (Tokyo: Dohbunkan, 1993b). See also *Strategic Budgeting*, 2nd Edition (Westport, CT and London: Quorum Books, Forthcoming).

Ishikawa, Akira and Ryuichiro Hirota, "ISOP: A Computerized Group-Based Intelligent Problem-Solving Technique," in *Proceedings of the 27th Annual Hawaii International Conference on System Sciences*, 1994, pp. 291–299.

Ishikawa, Akira and Hiroshi Mieno, "The Personnel Development System as a Negotiation Support System," in *Proceedings of the HICSS-25*, 1992, pp. 199–204.

Ishikawa, Akira, Hiroshi Mieno, and Rumi Tatsuta, "Knowledge Engineering Management — Issues and Prospects," *Human Systems Management*, Vol. 10, No. 2, 1991, pp. 141–148.

Ishikawa, Akira, Katsuhiro Sasaki, and Tetsuo Hirouchi, "Historical Backgrounds of Creativity Studies and Various Idea-Conceiving Methods (I)," *Operations Research* (Japan), Vol. 26, No. 5, 1981a, pp. 36–40.

Ishikawa, Akira, Katsuhiro Sasaki, and Tetsuo Hirouchi, "Historical Backgrounds of Creativity Studies and Various Idea-Conceiving Methods (II)," *Operations Research* (Japan), Vol. 26, No. 6, 1981b, pp. 41–48.

Katagata, Zenji and Nobuhiro Tajima, *An Introduction to ZK Method: Problem-Solving Methods by Full Participants* (Nihon Keieisha Dantai Renmei, 1978).

Kawakita, Jiro, *An Introduction to KJ Method* (Tokyo: Kodansha, 1975).

Matsuda, Takehiko, "Organizational Intelligence," in Akira Ishikawa and Kazuhiro Horiuchi (eds.), *Information Strategy in Global Management* (Tokyo: Yuuhikaku, 1994).

Mori, Tatsuo, *PERT* (Tokyo: Japan Management Association, 1964).

Nadler, Gerald, *Risosisutemu Sekkei: Work Design no atarashii Hatten*, trans. Ryuichi Yoshida (Tokyo: Toyokeizai Shimpo, 1969).

Nakamura, Nobuo, *An Introduction to Business Design Methods* (Tokyo: Japan Management Association, 1979).

Nakayama, Masakazu, *An Introduction to NM Method* (Tokyo: Sanno Univ. Press, 1965).

Nunamaker, J. F., Allan R. Dennis, Joseph S. Valacich, Douglas R. Vogel, and Joey F. George, "Electronic Meeting Systems to Support Group Work," *Communications of the ACM*, Vol. 34, No. 7, July 1991, p. 43.

Parnes, Sidney J. and Harold F. Harding (eds.), *A Source Book for Creative Thinking* (N.Y.: Scribners, 1962).

R&D Guidebook Editorial Committee (ed.), *Research and Development Guidebook* (Tokyo: JUSE, 1973), pp. 316, 329–331.

Rogers, Carl R., *Encounter Group: Ningen Shinrai no Genten wo motomete*, trans. M. Hatase (Tokyo: Diamond, 1973).

Rogers, Carl R., *Rogers Zenshu, 1966–1976* (Tokyo: Iwasaki Gakujutsu Press, 1987).

Siks, Geraldine Brain, *Kodomo no tameno Souzou Kyoiku*, trans. Akira Okada and Koichi Takahashi (Tokyo: Tamagawa University Press, 1973).

Takahashi, Hiroshi, *A New Method of Idea Creation* (Tokyo: Nihon Jitsugyo Shuppan, 1984).

Takahashi, Makoto, *How to Proceed with Conferences* (Tokyo: Japan Economic Newspaper, 1987).

Takahashi, Makoto, *50 Steps to Heighten Practical Design Capabilities* (Tokyo: Kou-Shobou, 1989a).

Takahashi, Makoto, *Knowledge of Problem-Solving Techniques* (Tokyo: Japan Economic Newspaper, 1989b).

Takahashi, Makoto, "Classification and Utilization of Creativity Techniques," in Makoto Takahashi (ed.), *Business Creation Bible* (Mode Gakuen Press, 1993), pp. 252–263.

Ueno, Ichiro, *Wisdom of Management: Brainstorming ABC* (Tokyo: Rokkou, 1959).

Umesao, Tadao, *Techniques for Intelligent Production* (Tokyo: Yuanami Shoten, 1989).

Whiting, C. S., *Creative Thinking* (New York: Reinhold, 1958).

Whiting, C. S., *Kigyou ni okeru Souzousei no Kaihatsu to Katsuyou*, trans. Minoru Kurumado (Tokyo: Diamond, 1963).

PART III

Chapter 11

Business Intelligence
and Its Practical Use

IBM began its Business Intelligence (BI) with the Global Business Intelligence Solution in 1995. In 1996, IBM Japan set up a BI Promotion Department, and started offering BI solutions. Since then, IBM has been developing a solution business that makes full use of BI functions. In this chapter, we will examine the theories and value of BI, citing various case examples.

1. Accumulating Internal Corporate Information

As corporate management has become more and more complex, it is no longer possible to steer a company by hunches and experience alone. Various management methods have been developed and are adopted in many companies. A data accumulation and management system is necessary for quantitative management of these methods. For example, with the introduction of ERP, business processing and the accompanying accounting information have become clearly visible, while widespread CRM now enables record-keeping of contacts with customers. In the manufacturing industry, SCM facilitates access to information relating to processes from raw material procurement and production, to shipment. Also, employees nowadays are given more training in relevant skills and competencies, so as to deepen their expertise for effective development of human resources. Thus, corporate information — ranging from that of accounting, of customers, of processes, to that of personnel — is now amassed as intelligence for each purpose. Therefore, systems for storing such information, and for utilizing it as intelligence, have been gradually developed. The data extraction and display system proposed by Gideon Gartner, for instance, is now available as a convenient BI tool, sold by various software companies.

Of particular note here is that in storing data and turning it into intelligence for corporate activities, there is a gap between the amount of data that could be made use of as intelligence, and the amount of data that is stored. This is called the Knowledge Gap. Many corporations and organizations face problems in utilizing their data assets, as they lack an analytical ability to effectively utilize accumulated data as intelligence, and are hence unable to turn data into knowledge and share it within the company. There are many examples of this: supermarkets with their POS data analysis, manufacturers unable to develop customer-oriented products due to lack of purchase information, financial institutions with their disproportionate financing and non-performing loans, and medical malpractice due to insufficient analysis of patient information. Therefore, the issue of how to reduce this Knowledge Gap may be the one big differentiator for companies.

CRM's customer contact history combines information from various sources, enabling an organization as a whole to deal with customers as one top salesperson or as a singular dependable point of contact. This system has been adopted by many companies, generally to the high satisfaction of their customers. On the other hand, do Marketing Customer Information Files (MCIF) of banks and customer information database of sales companies function as systems that allow corporate users to effectively grasp each individual customer?

It is highly questionable if corporations and organizations utilize intelligence based on an accurate understanding of customers' needs. Figure 10 shows the definition of corporations' customer-oriented knowledge. Knowledge that gives companies a competitive edge is knowledge that secures them high customer loyalty. It is crucial that companies learn how to acquire such knowledge.

For this purpose, companies need to have highly advanced data analysis systems and the relevant skills for using them. There are two

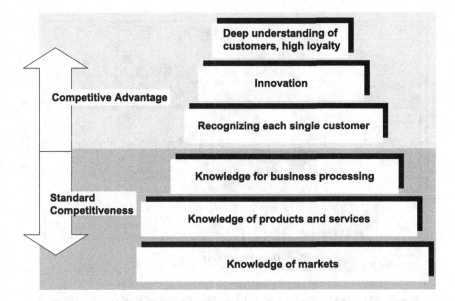

Figure 10:   Customer-Oriented Knowledge

types of accumulated data: numerical, categorical data and text data. The former is quantitative and can be analyzed numerically. The latter is hard to analyze numerically, and therefore requires a different kind of data analysis method. Data mining is commonly used for numerical, categorical data, while text mining is applied to text data. Statistical analysis algorithms have also been in use for many years, but their use tends to be limited to data analysts and scholars.

These data analysis techniques enable companies to turn data into intelligence, and then into knowledge. Thus, data analysis is a crucial source of differentiation for companies and organizations. IBM's data analysis techniques, i.e., its "Business Intelligence" (BI), are shown in Figure 11.

2. Basics of Knowledge Management

As per IBM's terminology, turning data into knowledge is called "knowledge management". As can be seen in Figure 12, IBM develops its knowledge technologies in five basic areas, and provides

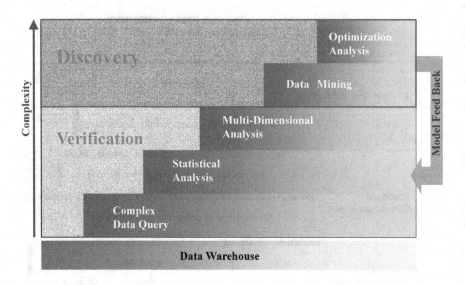

Figure 11: IBM's Definition of BI — Five Phases of Business Intelligence

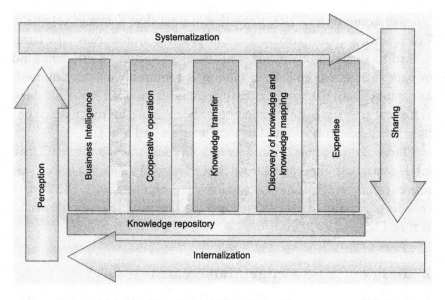

Figure 12: Five Basic Areas of Knowledge Management at IBM

solutions for business operations. BI is among those five basic areas of knowledge management, and IBM actively uses its five phases of BI (see Figure 11) as a vital part of the process of turning information into knowledge.

One of the basic techniques of BI is text mining, especially in relation to analysis of Japanese text data (see Figure 13). Text mining techniques are developed based on three basic functions:

(1) Natural Language Analysis and Concept Extraction
     Includes techniques such as morphological analysis, pattern analysis, keyword extraction, dictionaries, processing of diversity and ambiguity of expressions, unifying synonymous expressions, and categorizing techniques.
(2) Mining
     Includes information search technology, technology to analyze concepts from various perspectives and organize them, and technologies for identifying tendencies, phenomena, and correlations

What is Text Mining?
As it takes considerable time and effort to read stored texts so as to analyze and organize them, texts are quite often left abandoned.Text mining techniques offer effective tools and know-how for storing texts.

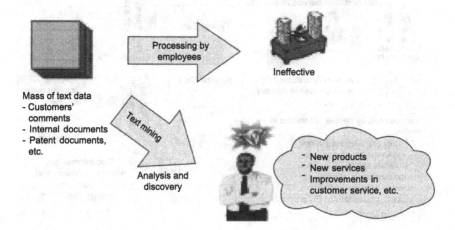

Figure 13:　Text Mining

of interest, such as frequency analysis, correlation analysis, and time-series analysis.

(3) Visualization and Dialogue Processing
Includes technologies for displaying analyzed and organized concepts graphically, and technologies for dialogue processing through graphic user interface.

All of these are combined into text mining technologies, which enable users to interpret text data and extract important information from texts. Figure 14 shows an example of how text mining is used to obtain knowledge at a PC's call center. Call center operators record claims from customers in the customers' own expressions; however, these may encompass various dialects and faulty expressions, and it may take considerable time and effort to organize such records in order to prepare standard replies. Typical data (i.e., numerical data) can be easily analyzed and stored, but text data (i.e., atypical data) tends to remain

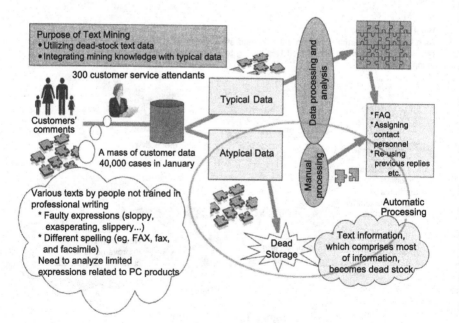

Figure 14: How to Obtain Knowledge Through Text Mining

untouched, without being organized properly. Text mining technologies make it possible to organize and analyze text data, by automatically sorting through text information and extracting important data from the mass of text data into other systems such as FAQ databases.

If we ask customers to leave comments on services or products, instead of asking them to grade them, we can learn their real opinions and assessments, which will make customer satisfaction surveys more accurate. Technologies for direct text mining from speeches — voice mining — have also been developed, and will soon become another strategic tool for obtaining knowledge.

3. Smart Use of Information is Vital for Corporate Management

As shown in Figure 15, corporate activities are controlled by three applications connecting consumers to suppliers: Supply Chain Management (SCM) — optimization from raw material procurement to production; Enterprise Resource Planning (ERP) — standardization of internal systems; and Customer Relationship Management (CRM) — customer management and optimization of sales. Most major corporations adopt these three applications, using BI to analyze accumulated data. That is to say, BI exists not only as a system on its own, but it is also incorporated into various solutions as an engine for obtaining knowledge.

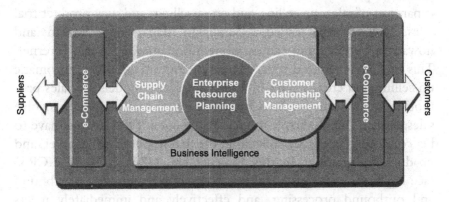

Figure 15:　Process and Application Integration

3.1. *CRM and BI*

The area of corporate management where BI is most actively used is, perhaps, customer management. In this section, we will examine how information is utilized in CRM. Customer management started to prevail in Japan in 1997. Whereas previously Total Quality Control (TQC) was all the vogue, Japanese companies that prosper nowadays are fully engaged in CRM, placing it at the base of corporate management as part of the Customer Satisfaction Movement.

CRM, as shown in Figure 16, stores and organizes customer information gained through direct contact with customers, thereby building a CRM database. It therefore helps to instill in salespeople a deep and accurate understanding of customers that is cultivated from customer contact history.

CRM can be divided into Operational CRM, which is based in call centers (or contact centers) and functions as the contact points for customers, and Analytical CRM, which is based in the back office and provides analyses of accumulated data for determining sales policies. Thus, CRM is a form of BI in that it is truly the brains behind highly customized sales.

As the term "database marketing" denotes, it is now possible to plan, execute and evaluate marketing policies based on accumulated data by using BI. For CRM to identify each individual customer, various data must be ascribed to each customer type in order to build a customer profile data. Accumulation of such data contributes to expansion of sales, up-selling and cross-selling, and new product trial sales. This system is called a Campaign Management System, and nowadays campaigning can be done automatically via the Internet. This in turn is referred to as Marketing Automation, i.e., automatic up-selling and cross-selling by using predictive models for sales promotion built from purchase history. This process does not involve salespeople. The predictive models at the core of this process have to be constantly updated, reflecting the latest purchase, market and product information. In this Internet era, CRM is called e-CRM (see Figure 17) — a system that automates web handling of inbound and outbound processing, and effectively and immediately meets

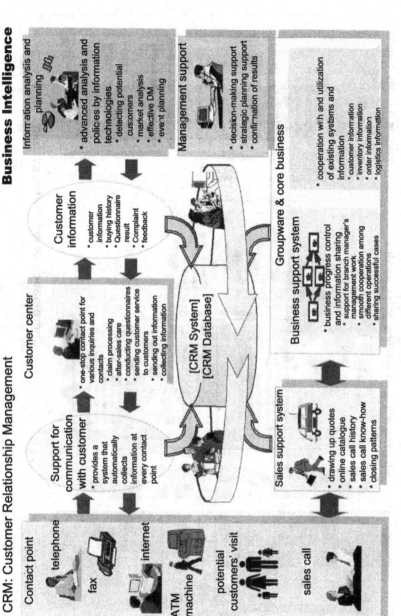

Figure 16: CRM and BI

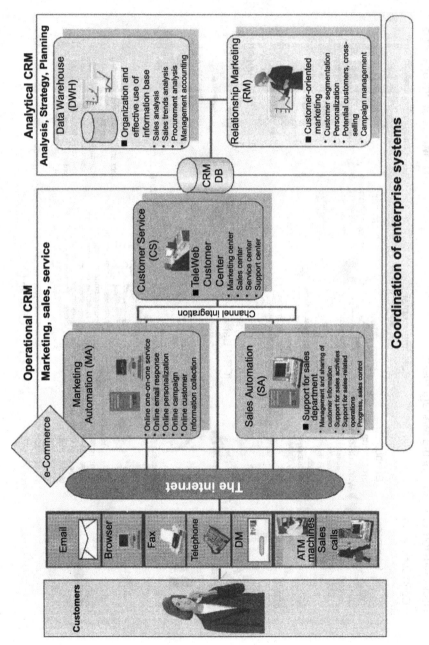

Figure 17: e-CRM

customers' requests. Event-Based Marketing automatically detects changes in customer behavior, and adopts the best possible measures in response. Many corporations have already started to adopt e-CRM as a differentiated sales strategy.

3.2. *BSC and BI*

From management's point of view, money matters such as budget control and financial management are important. With the advent of the Balanced Score Card (BSC) approach, it has become highly necessary to quantitatively control the corporate strategy execution process for hypothesis testing. Thus, corporate financial decision-making involves not only management considerations; advanced analysis techniques, especially those of statistical analysis and data mining, have to be taken into account too.

It therefore goes without saying that BI is important for business. In almost all areas of corporate activities, BI is needed, and finding such needs and adopting BI as a system should become the corporate strategy itself. Differentiation will depend on how well a company performs this task.

4. Cases of Business Intelligence in Use

Figure 18 lists a few examples of IBM's use of BI for problem solving. Data mining techniques, in particular, are featured heavily.

In this section, we will examine some case studies of various BI solutions. Table 5 provides a summary of the case studies profiled here and the BI functions involved.

4.1. *Manufacturing*

a. *Corporation A — air-conditioner manufacturer*

As it was impossible to predict demand conditions for winter, Corporation A based its product manufacturing plan for winter on the sales department's order estimate in the summertime. The company

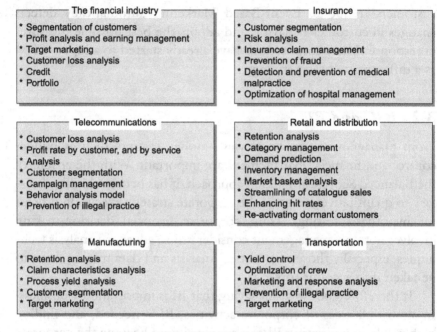

Figure 18:   IBM's BI Cases by Industry

needed to send in orders for parts three months before shipment. Therefore, in order to determine the optimum order, Corporation A needed an optimum demand forecast for optimum production planning. It was not possible, however, to predict demand accurately based on past sales records and sales plans. This was made especially tricky because of recent abnormal weather patterns like El Niño which caused an unusually cool summer; there was a danger that air conditioners might not sell as well as planned, leaving a mass of stock behind.

In order to cope with this situation, the production planning department studied various methods of demand forecasting, and decided to develop a demand forecasting system that incorporated advanced BI. Apart from internal data such as production and sales data, external data, including the number of new homes being built, industrial production index, and weather data, are now used for demand forecasting too. Based on such data, accuracy is greatly

Table 5: Actual Cases and Used BI Functions

BI cases	Data search	Statistics analysis	Online Analytical Processing (OLAP)	Data mining	Optimization analysis
A	O	O		O	O
B	O	O		O	O
C	O	O		O	
OMC Card	O	O		O	
Cecile	O	O		O	O
The Sumitomo Trust and Banking	O	O	O	O	
Meiji Life Insurance Company	O	O		O	
D	O	O	O	O	
Nagasaki Medical Center	O	O		O	
Japan Racing Association	O	O		O	
E	O	O	O		

enhanced now (below 10%), e.g., by predicting shipment trends through statistical analysis, and by minimizing error through data mining techniques (see Figure 19).

b. *Corporation B — steel maker*

Corporation B was engaged in providing overseas clients with designed parts for giant marine constructs. One time, one of its clients pointed out that part of the steel material delivered was found to be unacceptable after a sample test, and requested re-delivery of all the goods. As Corporation B had thorough quality control, the technical manager found it hard to believe that the goods delivered did not meet the requirements, and so decided to examine why and how some goods were unacceptable. The company employed IBM's BI analyst to

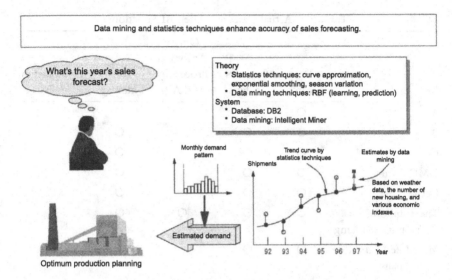

Figure 19: Electronics Manufacturer's Case — Demand Forecasting

conduct data analysis. The IBM analyst used IBM's data mining tool, Intelligent Miner, to analyze data from all the production processes, and discovered that most of the samples used for the sample test showed different attributes from all the other delivered goods. After explaining this to the client, Corporation B was able to exchange newly-produced goods only for the faulty ones used in the sample test, instead of re-delivering all the goods, the lost profits of which would have been about four billion yen. Since then, many engineers have learnt this data mining technique for quality control (see Figure 20).

c. *Corporation C — new product development by a food manufacturer*

Corporation C, a bread manufacturer, needed to develop a new product and sell it to a major supermarket that it had an ongoing relationship with. Corporation C was able to obtain bread sales data regularly, so it could analyze the sales trends. It could also control the production process and ingredient combination data through its affiliated factories.

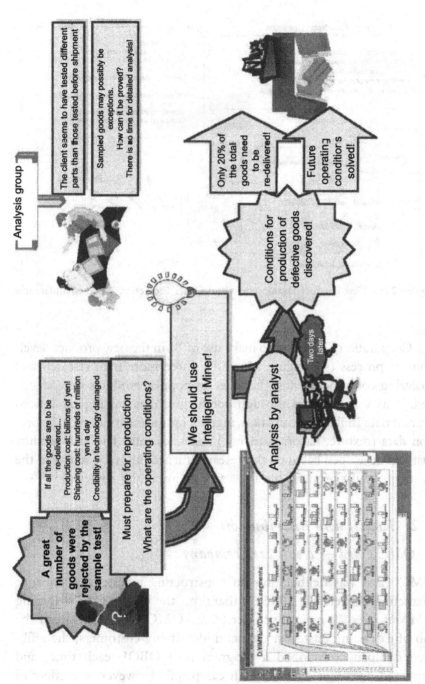

Figure 20: Example of Quality Control: Industrial Goods

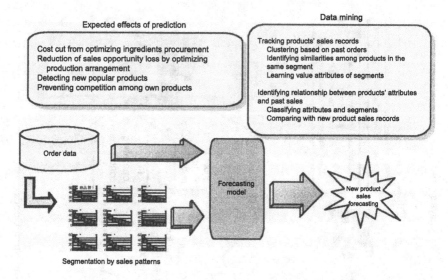

Figure 21:   New Product Development and Order Prediction: Food Manufacturer

Corporation C decided to make use of BI in the new product development process (see Figure 21). After three months of research and analyzing consumer trends, the traits for popular products were identified. This was achieved through conducting data mining on various process data (milling information, ingredients information, etc.), inspection data (texture, flavor, taste, etc.) and sales data. The new product that was developed based on this research turned out to be similar to the existing popular product, but it became an instant hit anyway.

4.2. *Retail and distribution*

a. *OMC Card — credit card company*

OMC Card was deliberating on constructing a system to enhance marketing efficiency in 1996. At that time, the IT cost for distributing DM was over 20 million yen per batch. OMC Card outsourced the job of extracting customer data and identifying customers; the affiliated company developed a program by COBOL each time, and extracted customer data for each campaign. However, the effect of campaigning could only be surmised, based on sales information from existing legacy systems. Identification of customers was insufficiently handled, and the same DM could be sent to customers multiple times, or to customers who expressly did not want them.

In order to solve these problems, OMC Card decided to develop a Campaign Management System. After examining both domestic and foreign solutions, it decided to develop its own system, and a project team was formed. Consisting of elites from the marketing department and the systems department, they established and defined the necessary requirements after three months of discussion. IBM Japan's Tokyo Research Laboratory then started developing Campaign Manager. After another three months, identification of customers and compiling of a database were finished, and Campaign Manager was completed (see Figure 22).

Campaign Manager extracts the results of customer segmentation by IBM's Intelligent Miner into DM lists for different types of campaigns, and sends out DM to customers. The effectiveness of each campaign is measured by each campaign's code, and is recorded in the CRM database. This system enables OMC Card to conduct campaigns 20 times a year, ten times more frequently than before, and to measure their effect quantitatively; this clearly shows the ROI of developing such a system.

Campaign Manager was further improved in 2004, and now, in cooperation with OMC Card's credit risk management system (see Figure 23), it has become a very effective one-to-one marketing system. In short, it has turned into a strategic marketing system that manages diversified campaigns over a hundred times a year, and is capable of conducting test marketing.

b. *Cecile — major catalog retailer*

The major catalog retailer Cecile adopted IBM's DB2 and Intelligent Miner, with the aim of building a customer database and grasping individual customers' buying trends, in order to make singular categorical catalogs more accurately targeted at customers' preferences, so as to achieve one-to-one marketing (see Figure 24). The hardware

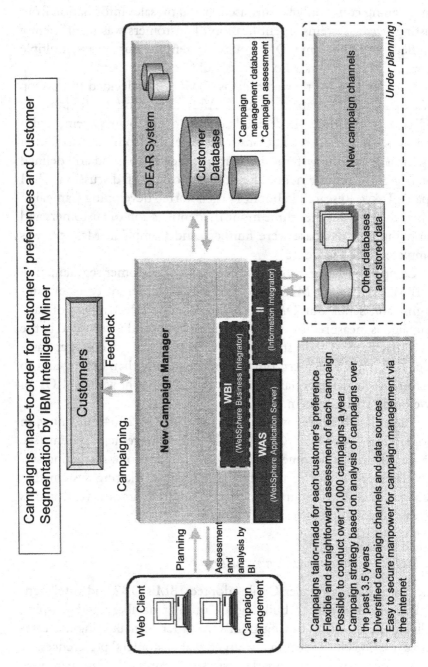

Figure 22: OMC Card's New Campaign Management System

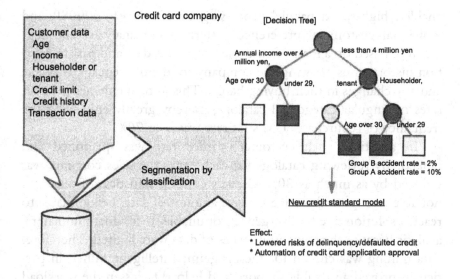

Figure 23: Example of Credit Risk Management by Card Approval Modeling

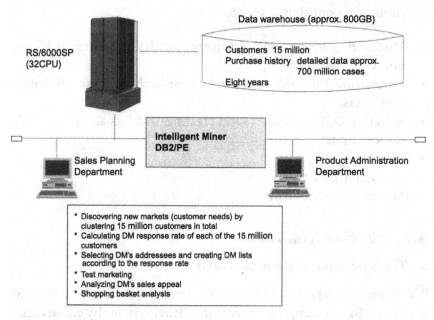

Figure 24: Cecile — Example of Advanced One-to-One Marketing by Data Mining

enabled high-speed parallel processing by IBM's RS/6000SP, and individual customers' preference patterns were analyzed and segmented, based on a mass of customer attributes data and past transaction history, thus allowing the company to identify repeat customers and any changes in their buying habits. This in turn enhanced the hit rates of singular categorical catalogs, thereby greatly enhancing the frequency of repurchase. DM's hit rate was over 70%.

In addition, each customer's order rate was quantified and ranked. By reviewing catalogs for each rank, the sales cost rate was reduced by as much as 30%. Cecile's existing statistics software was not able to cope with such a massive amount of data, being unable to reach a solution due to divergences, or unable to conduct multilateral analysis because the compatible types of data were limited. Therefore, data mining was chosen for the program; Intelligent Miner, in particular, proved a valuable support, and helped to lessen the workload for analysts and salespeople.

Cecile's Sales Planning Department has achieved the following, which in turn contributed to sales promotion:

- Discovering new markets (customer needs) by clustering 15 million customers in total;
- Calculating the DM response rate of each of these 15 million customers;
- Selecting DM's addressees and creating DM lists according to the response rate;
- Test marketing;
- Analyzing DM's sales appeal;
- Shopping basket analysis.

4.3. *The financial industry*

a. *The Sumitomo Trust and Banking*

The Sumitomo Trust and Banking has been developing an innovative Customer Relationship Management (CRM) system, by constructing a new customer database and expanding its customer contact centers. The bank uses the basic BI of Marketing Customer Information

File (MCIF), a business solution developed by IBM, to understand customer trends in its quest to become the customers' ideal bank. Figure 25 shows how the various customer contact points, the customer database, and the accounting and information databases are integrated at Sumitomo.

The Sumitomo Trust and Banking conducted a drastic overhaul of its marketing system from 1996 to 1999 (see Figure 26). The manager of the Project Planning Department, Tomimatsu, said, "We learned that it wasn't necessarily best to provide all our customers with the same products; so we made a fundamental change to our policy. Now we are able to offer customers services and products that are custom-made for their needs the moment when these needs arise during our customers' lifecycle, thanks to our technology."

By making use of Marketing Customer Information File (MCIF), The Sumitomo Trust and Banking was able to reconstruct customer data into valuable data. Currently, branches share data with each other, including customers' personal and family information. All branches have sufficient and full-functioning tools for direct marketing. When used for marketing campaigns, such data allow the bank to capture the targets more securely. Since the new system was introduced, The Sumitomo Trust and Banking has been able to identify business trends more accurately than ever before.

Machida, the then manager of the Project Planning Department, said, "Our clients' needs differ according to their lifestyle, life stages, age, and other various factors. By utilizing IBM's solution, now we can view things scientifically, and consequently, we are able to conduct excellent CRM that can recognize extremely elusive differences in human behavior."

The information obtained through this BI solution is utilized in all CRM areas, such as establishing new business, cross-selling, customer retention, enhancement of campaign management efficiency, introduction of incentives necessary for obtaining new customers by buzz marketing, etc. As Machida explains, "We can analyze data to see if we have fewer transactions with a certain client than before. If we learn that that's the case, we notify the salespeople in charge, and they immediately execute sales strategy for related products."

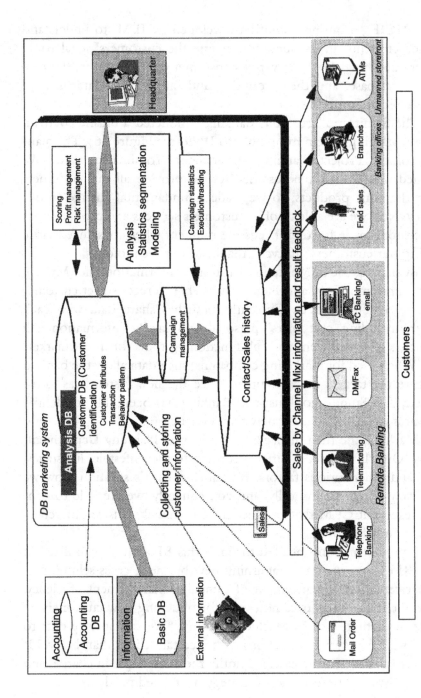

Figure 25: The Sumitomo Trust and Banking: Introduction of BI

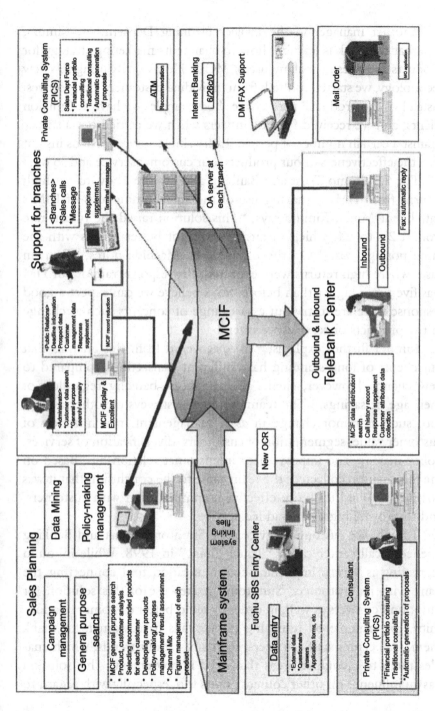

Figure 26: Marketing System at The Sumitomo Trust and Banking

Another manager in the Project Planning Department, Kimura, says that the bank is learning how to change its marketing strategy for products and sales by making use of MCIF. He says, "By using this new technology, we started to think from individual customers' perspectives, instead of the products' perspective. For example, we have 1.7 million clients, and we received 92,000 answers when we carried out a survey against a certain number of people. Every single answer gave us insight into the effectiveness of our products, our customer service and so on."

The Sumitomo Trust and Banking also explored how to get high returns from DM by making use of the analytic functions of IBM's Intelligent Miner. Kimura says, "This solution raised the return rate from 1.2% to 6%, which means that we got better results with the same postage cost." On the other hand, Machida notes, "Even in cases where high returns were expected, the response rate of our DM was five times higher than before. So, I believe we can expect a good response if we are to try out a vast range of concepts such as change in the products or services we offer."

Kimura further explains, "We discovered from this analysis that our clients of long-standing have different transactions compared to new clients. However, clients use telephone banking regardless of their age or savings." The team conducted surveys on other aspects too, such as minor change in asset management, maximization of customer value, segmentation of customers, diversification of services, policy-making, and improvement in customer relationship. Based on the information collected, the team came to the conclusion that it was possible to build up more effective communication with customers, and to provide high value-added service.

To enhance customer service, The Sumitomo Trust and Banking opened a call center called "Touch Point" in 1998. While inbound marketing is a very important communication tool connecting the bank with its customers, Sumitomo makes use of this solution for outbound contacts as well, in order to build better customer relationships, for example by returning phone calls to customers to thank them. Call center staff can keep records of various trends, which enables them to recognize areas that need improvement. This solution has an influence on other contact points too, especially with regard to

Internet banking. The bank's Internet banking team is planning to make several changes within the year to meet the needs of customers who prefer Internet banking to other contact methods, so that they will have improved access to account information and balance data.

Normally, the information that banks have is limited to the data that customers provide them with. However, in the case of Sumitomo, the data obtained from MCIF analysis are sent to different customer segments as messages; then, based on the customer replies, the bank discusses and analyzes the various issues including if slogans are appropriate, if colors and sizes are effective, if texts are best suited for the campaign, if advertisements are effective, and customers' feedback regarding yet-to-be-released products and already well-established products. Thus, MCIF contributes to building up practical and effective business.

Tomimatsu notes, "If I give just one reason for our choosing IBM, it's the people. Data analysis means nothing if it doesn't lead to action. When selecting a vendor, the assessment criterion is whether they can provide us with the solution we need or not. With IBM, we knew immediately that we could translate newly gained data into action using IBM's solution."

The Sumitomo Trust and Banking is one of the major institutional investors in Japan, with investments of approximately 12 trillion yen. The bank has a very strong bond with its customers, and the total assets of over 30 trillion yen deposited in the bank is proof of this strong trust. The Sumitomo Trust and Banking is also ranked number one among commercial and industrial real estate brokers.

The Sumitomo Trust and Banking is engaged in a wide range of major businesses including asset management, pension trust funds, corporate financing, retail, real estate business, and overseas bases. The bank has a network of over 30 major markets worldwide, and has established a secure position as one of the leading asset management companies in the world.

Its MCIF Project was started in 1998 and was completed in 1999. Machida recollects, "Even before our partnership with IBM started, we did know the concepts of such solutions. But working with the experts from IBM broadened our views, and helped deepen our understanding of what we were aiming to do."

The MCIF Project provided the bank with various new processing abilities that it did not possess before. All marketing teams were given access to MCIF; consequently, all the branches, call centers, and planning teams that were involved in marketing were linked, and business operation information at the bank headquarters was also shared with them. Based on the single platform of MCIF, the entire network of the bank gained unlimited power of data storage and retrieval. The bank's customers benefited as well from easy and swift access to account and related information via various channels.

What changes did IBM's solution bring to business operations at The Sumitomo Trust and Banking? Machida explains, "We've already seen some big changes in our business operations. Each branch can freely use information without depending on others. Since they are given easy access to information, a healthy competition among branches is born. This is because, although branches are located in separate areas, this solution helped us establish a system where all branches are given the same information feedback."

The new technology strengthened Sumitomo's relationship with its customers, and greatly expanded the bank's business prospects. This new system benefits customers at all levels, instead of making a noticeable difference in service for the most important customers only. Tomimatsu concludes, "We have been given access to the world of highly valuable information and insight. Now we can decide on the best method of communication with each segment of customers, and the most valuable products and services for each customer group, using scientific methods. This new technology has allowed us to put customers first in anything we do."

4.4. *Insurance*

a. *Customer data management system at Meiji Life Insurance Company*

When the insurance market in Japan was de-regulated, Meiji Life Insurance Company (now Meiji Yasuda Life Insurance Company, after a merger with Yasuda Life Insurance Company) faced a dilemma of how to improve sales productivity. The company was especially worried that it would not be easy to compete against foreign insurance companies with various insurance products and knowledgeable salespeople.

Therefore, it decided to establish a customer database similar to that being introduced in banks, and to start promoting online transaction by DM, leading to the establishment of a one-to-one marketing system. Meiji Life Insurance Company believed that in establishing and maintaining good customer relations through DM and the Internet, it is imperative that each service is provided personally by each salesperson. Therefore, in order to build a mutually beneficial relationship, Meiji decided to introduce a data mining system that would enable it to better understand each customer's attributes, and that would enable salespeople to suggest products best suited for each customer.

This system allowed the company to learn a great deal about customers in various life stages. Most notably, it enabled the company to develop and offer insurance products more suited for old people in their various life circumstances. This led to a hit product called Life Account.

IBM's business intelligence solution was indeed the turning point for Meiji Life Insurance Company to become a customer-oriented company.

4.5. *Telecommunications*

a. *Corporation D — securing customer share*

Price wars have become common in today's saturated telecommunications market; however, most telecommunication companies do not have enough new subscribers to cover the cut-down in prices, and bills per month and per customer are on the decline. For Corporation D, apart from maintaining its market share, the big issue for improving its sales is not losing heavy users and promoting more frequent use, besides working on light users.

With the help of IBM's BI consultant, Corporation D established a point of reference for dividing its customers into different segments and managing them by segment, by applying the data mining technology to its customer information database. Corporation D also built a discriminant model for analyzing cancellations of contracts, so that it could detect signs of customers considering cancellation of their contracts, as well as a discriminant model for exploring which customer segment would be most likely to transfer to another segment. Discriminant models were tested thoroughly against detailed telephone bills, service logs and sales information, and were built into the business system so that they could provide guidance in the ordinary course of business (see Figure 27). Through further in-depth analysis, these discriminant models can help prevent future cancellation of contracts and make existing customers more profitable. The steps involved are as follows. First, the necessary data is extracted from the data warehouse where transaction history and customer information are stored, and a data mart is built on IBM's UDB. Data mining is then conducted using IBM Intelligent Miner's bivariate statistics, decision tree, and classification function. Finally, suggestions for necessary business moves are made, executed, and the company's market share is thus secured.

4.6. *Healthcare*

a. *National Hospital Organization, Nagasaki Medical Center*

Nagasaki Medical Center published its hepatic disease and liver cancer patients' death prediction model, which was built using data mining techniques, in March 2004. Prediction was based on analysis of the blood test results of hepatic disease and liver cancer patients.

Based on this prediction model, it was recognized that the test items — liver tumor markers and liver reserve — have a strong connection to patients' survival. Especially among liver cancer patients, liver tumor markers' absolute values are closely connected with survival and life expectancy. This model can now be used to predict liver cancer and hepatic disease patients' life expectancy and survival time, and is expected to provide guidance on the choice and assessment of treatment, including medical transplants.

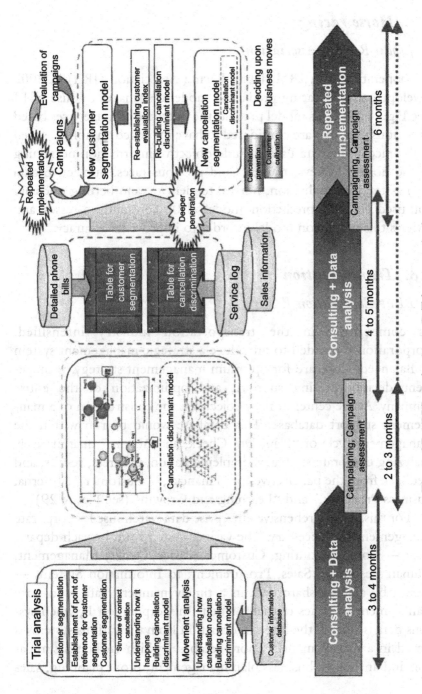

Figure 27: BI Introduction at D Telecommunications

4.7. *Horse racing*

a. *Japan Racing Association*

In cooperation with IBM, Japan Racing Association (JRA) in 2002 developed a horse racing prediction model that makes full use of BI (see Figure 28). This model predicts the outcome of horse races based on various data that are considered to have influence on horses' speed in the races. The data used include objective information pertaining to the horses, jockeys, trainers, and previous races. Subjective data such as trainers' evaluation, horses' tendencies, and betting odds are not used for this prediction model. JRA constantly assesses and reviews this prediction model in order to improve its accuracy.

4.8. *Transportation*

a. *BI at Corporation E*

As competition in the transportation industry intensified, Corporation E decided to introduce a strategic management system by Balanced Scorecard for optimum management strategy, management decision-making support, and optimization of the entire company. At the center of this project was the construction of a management support database. This database would be run within the management cycle of "Plan, Do, Check, and Action," quantitatively analyzing corporate strategies' implementation, progress, results, and feedback from the perspectives of "Financial," "Customer," "Internal Business Processes," and "Learning and Growth" (see Figure 29).

For this, a comprehensive enterprise data warehouse for corporate management was necessary. The various systems run by each department — from Accounting, Customer Service, Quality Management, Human Resources, Sales, Procurement, to Information Systems — should be able to share data in a timely manner. Data repository management becomes crucial for that. In Corporation E, when systems data is shared, the latest information from the various systems is stored in a management support database, which facilitates simulation and analysis of business plan management, profit planning, sales

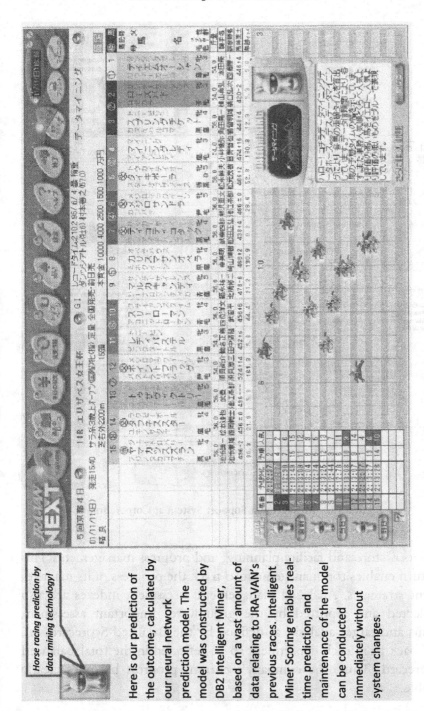

Horse racing prediction by data mining technology!

Here is our prediction of the outcome, calculated by our neural network prediction model. The model was constructed by DB2 Intelligent Miner, based on a vast amount of data relating to JRA-VAN's previous races. Intelligent Miner Scoring enables real-time prediction, and maintenance of the model can be conducted immediately without system changes.

Figure 28: JRA-VAN NEXT — Prediction Page

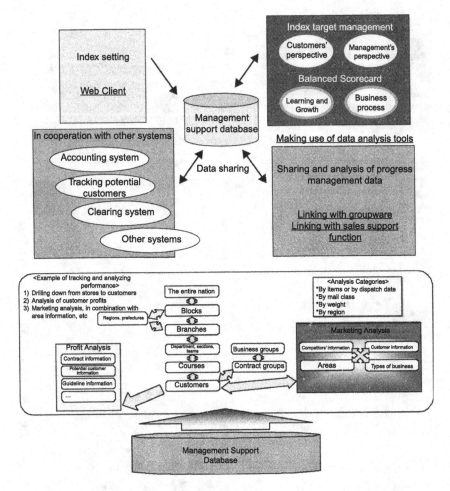

Figure 29: Management Support System at Corporation E

support, store and facility planning, and progress management. This in turn enables top management to track the progress of its management strategies. Analyzed management assessment indexes are also collected and reported by the groupware. Important assessment items and target analysis, as defined by the Balanced Scorecard, are fed back from each department to be reflected in the total Balanced Scorecard. Thus, the company's current progress becomes clearly visible.

Corporation E has set up a project team that encompasses the entire company; with the team's budget already incorporated into the company's medium-term management plan, Corporation E is well-placed to implement the project plan.

5. Summary

According to a survey conducted by IBM Japan's marketing division in 2000, only one out of seven people had heard of the term "Business Intelligence" (BI), and even then without much knowledge of what it meant. The recent usage of the term "BI" seems to have departed from its original meaning. In this chapter, I avoided cases of BI that involved simple Data Query/Reporting, because the purpose of this chapter is to show how Business Intelligence can lead to solutions for management problems.

Business solutions such as CRM, ERP, and SCM all share an element of BI. Nowadays, BI enables companies to differentiate themselves from competitors. It is not only about mere analysis; BI is also very much about turning a highly complex system into easy routine work, and incorporating it into the business system to make it available to end-users.

As information technology becomes even more advanced and data analysis makes implicit knowledge clearly visible, I believe that the use of BI should also evolve, as BI offers support to business professionals on all levels for optimum decision-making. For example, as On-Demand business continues to prosper with the explosive growth of the Internet, new technologies and software will be developed for instant analysis of massive and complex data, such as a vast amount of customer data, transaction data, and individual customers' preference data; and new marketing methods that make use of such technologies will undoubtedly be developed too. Furthermore, in the medical industry, there is a wide range of areas — from biogenetics, drug discovery, to medical treatment — where BI can be actively used. Thus, BI can contribute to all areas, not just business; and it is hoped that BI will spread to further fields of study as well.

Chapter 12

Strategy in Military History and Intelligence Activities in War

1. Introduction

1.1. *What is military history?*

Captain Sir Basil Liddell Hart, a British military scholar who served as an army captain in World War I, once noted that it is the fate of a soldier to be thrown into the battlefield one day, without any prior notice or experience. What he really means here is that, in addition to tactical exercises, soldiers should be trained in battlefield simulation by studying the history of past operations and battles.

Compared to politicians and businessmen, soldiers rarely experience critical situations unless they are already engaged in war. Therefore, by learning the history of warfare, soldiers aim to extract knowledge from past wars, extracting lessons from the past victories (successes) and defeats (failures). This is why the study of military history is so highly valued at military academies and in Japan's Self-Defense Forces.

In this chapter, we will try to grasp the realities of military intelligence activities in actual operations and battles through studying the history of warfare. Some readers may think that military intelligence activities are quite different from the day-to-day experience of the business world. There are, however, some common factors between war and business, and I believe it will benefit businesspeople to study military history.

1.2. What are "military intelligence activities"?

The purpose of military intelligence activities is to minimize the unknown factors related to the enemy and the combat areas, in order to help commanders assess the situation accurately and make the right tactical decisions. Intelligence activities typically consist of the following four processes, which are conducted simultaneously, continually and cyclically, and none of them can be omitted. They more or less correspond to the four methodologies of historical research, also shown below.

The four processes of intelligence activities are:

♦   Deciding what information is needed;
♦   Collecting information;
♦   Processing information (transforming data into intelligence);
♦   Making use of intelligence.

The above processes result in Assessment, Reporting and Distribution.
The four methodologies of historical research are:

♦   Identifying the research subject;
♦   Collecting materials;
♦   Examining the materials (verifying the historical facts);
♦   Making use of the historical facts.

The end result would be a research paper (historical investigation), or a presentation at an academic conference.

Although very similar, there are certain differences between intelligence activities and the methodologies of historical research. In the former, the timeliness of reporting is valued most, rather than the complete accuracy of the content, and untimely reporting, no matter how thorough, is considered to be of no use. On the other hand, there is nothing more important than thoroughness in historical research.

Another difference lies in the degree of difficulty in information processing and investigation of historical sources. It is extremely difficult to judge if a certain piece of intelligence is a "signal" or merely "noise" and to determine what it signifies while processing the information, but there is no such difficulty in investigation of historical sources, as historical events are already known facts. There is a big difference between historical investigation that can benefit from "hindsight," and intelligence activities that have to take a "stab in the dark," as it were.

Let us now take a look at the four processes of intelligence activities.

2. Four Processes of Intelligence Activities

Military intelligence activities can be broadly divided into strategic intelligence activities and tactical intelligence activities. With the former, it is necessary to clarify the intention of the target country's political leader, whereas with the latter, it is the military capacity of the target country that has to be verified. In this section, we will examine tactical intelligence activities at the level of combat troops or fleets whose principal task is to carry out operations and to engage in combat.

2.1. *Deciding what information is needed*

First, the commander must determine what the information requirements are for ascertaining the enemy troop's possible action, so that intelligence activities can be set in motion. Next, intelligence officers have to decide on the signs and information items that will best meet the commander's information requirements, consult their intelligence abilities, select the agency for collecting those items, set a plan for the project, and issue orders and instructions.

2.2. *Collecting information*

Intelligence agents systematically explore various sources of information, obtain information, and report it accordingly.

2.3. *Processing information (transforming data into intelligence)*

In this process, which consists of documentation, assessment, and judgment, the collected information is turned into intelligence. Generally, the procedure is as follows. First, the relevance of the collected information is examined. Then, the collected information items are sorted for convenience of the subsequent steps. Next, reliability of the sources and of the agents (i.e., their training, experience, ability, and likelihood of success) is reviewed. Following this, the accuracy of the information is examined by assessing its probability in comparison with other pieces of information already in possession. Finally, the information is analyzed, compared, and combined, and thus turned into intelligence that contributes to tactical decision-making.

What is vital in this process is discernment in judging information, sound judgment and logical thinking.

2.4. *Making use of intelligence*

The commander and the intelligence staff make use of the generated intelligence in order to assess the situation and combat area, and for intelligence estimation and reporting. The intelligence staff conducts intelligence estimation to satisfy the intelligence requirements from the top. The points that are usually covered in intelligence estimation can be summarized thus:

- Enemy's potential moves. If possible, rank them in order of probability.
- Enemy's potential moves which might gravely influence the mission (for avoiding a surprise attack).
- Enemy's weakness that can be taken advantage of.

3. The Battle of Midway in the Asia-Pacific War — the Pacific Campaign of World War II

In this section, we will examine the Battle of Midway in the Asia-Pacific War, as an example of military history. The Asia-Pacific War broke out on December 8, 1941 (the Pearl Harbor bombing), when Japan entered into war against the US, the UK and the Netherlands. The battlefield of the Asia-Pacific War could be divided into the Asian theater, where Japan's principal enemy was China, and the Pacific theater, where Japan's principal enemy was the US.

Figure 30 illustrates the Japanese control of the Pacific Ocean throughout the course of the Asia-Pacific War. The solid line in the middle of the West Pacific Ocean (stretching from Hainan Island, the Bashi Channel, the Marianas, Wake Island, to the Northern Kurile Islands) indicates the areas under the control of the Japanese Imperial Navy at the outbreak of the war, while the double solid line on the outer edge indicates the areas which Japan gained control over in the early offensive operations (approximately three to five months after

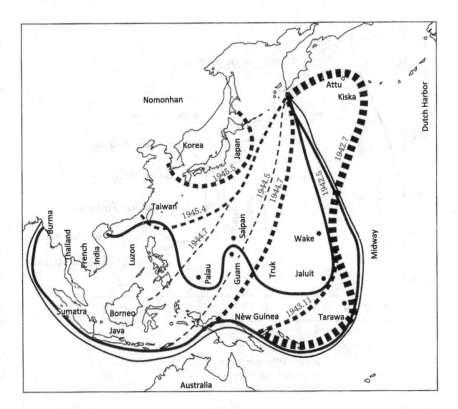

Figure 30:   The Japanese Control of the Pacific Ocean during the Asia-Pacific War

the war began). The thick dotted line crossing over the double solid line indicates the areas where the Japanese troops gained ground or withdrew from during the Midway and Aleutian operations and the Guadalcanal campaign. Meanwhile, the five dotted lines show how Japan, on the defensive, retreated further and further until the four Japanese islands were cornered within the thick dotted line.

Figure 31 illustrates the Japanese power curve in the Pacific Ocean throughout the course of the Asia-Pacific War. The vertical axis indicates the change in the areas under Japanese control, with the areas at the outset of the war set as 100. The horizontal axis represents the timeframe of the three years and eight months, from the start to the end of the war.

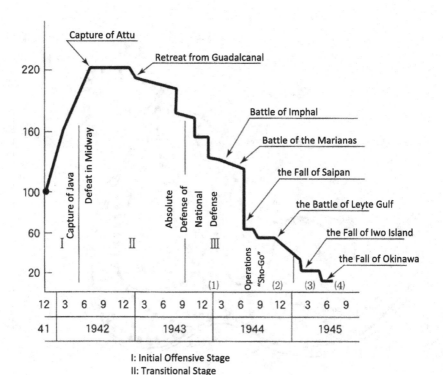

I: Initial Offensive Stage
II: Transitional Stage
III: Defensive Stage

Figure 31: The Japanese Power Curve in the Pacific Ocean

Figure 32 illustrates the General Principles of the War Direction, as decided in the Imperial Headquarters and the Government Liaison Conference ("Daihonei-Seihu Renrakukaigi") on March 7, 1942. The initial offensive operations, which the Imperial General Headquarters (IGHQ) had planned carefully, bore results that far exceeded expectations, and led the IGHQ to decide on a new policy: "In order to defeat Great Britain and deprive the US of the will to fight, we will expand the obtained military gains continuously, make preparations for unbroken victory, and take aggressive action, taking advantage of opportunities."

This was a hodgepodge of operations; a compromise between the Navy General Staff (N: "expand the obtained military gains continuously"), the Army General Staff (A: "make preparations for unbroken victory"), and the Grand Fleet Headquarters of the Imperial Japanese Navy (GF: "take aggressive action, taking advantage of opportunities"), which was subordinate to the Navy General Staff. These three organizations, with their three very different ideas, led the next phase of military operations into complete chaos, beginning with the simultaneous implementation of the Midway and the Aleutian operations.

The Midway operation began on June 5, 1942, just half a year after the outbreak of the war. As a result of the surprise attack on Pearl Harbor, where eight main battleships of the US Pacific Ocean Fleet had been sunk or destroyed, the relative position of Japan compared to the US had improved dramatically. The Imperial Japanese Navy (IJN) now held an advantage in both quality and quantity in the Pacific.

However, the three US aircraft carriers which the IJN missed in Pearl Harbor continued to carry out hit-and-run, guerrilla-style tactics, avoiding a decisive battle against the IJN. This caused major problems for Admiral Isoroku Yamamoto, the Commander-in-Chief of the Grand Fleet. Moreover, the new policy of the General Principles of the War Direction (see Figure 32) led the IJN to simultaneously implement both the Midway operation in the mid-Pacific and the Aleutian operation in the Northern Pacific Ocean. This meant dividing the dominant but limited powers of the IJN, and thus went against some of the most important warfare principles such as "establishment of united goals and objectives" and "concentration of forces."

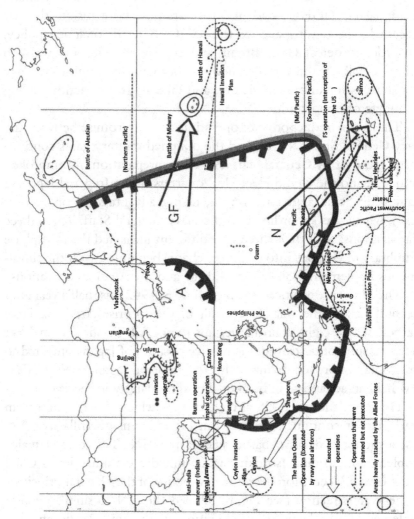

Figure 32: The General Principles of the War Direction

The Battle of Midway lasted over ten hours from sunrise to sunset on June 5, 1942 (see Figure 33); the IJN fought against three US aircraft carriers only to suffer a crushing defeat, losing four of its own aircraft carriers instead. There were many causes for this defeat, but the main one was the fatal tactical mistake made in the intelligence activities. In the following, we will study the tactical intelligence activities in the Battle of Midway by examining the commands of Vice-Admiral Chuichi Nagumo, Commander-in-Chief of the First Mobile Fleet, and the intelligence work of Nagumo's HQ.

4. Case Study: Intelligence Activities in the Battle of Midway

Of the "four processes of intelligence activities" mentioned earlier, this section covers three of them: deciding what information is needed, collecting information, and especially, processing information. The last process — making use of intelligence — will be summarized in Section 5 of this chapter.

4.1. *What were Vice-Admiral Nagumo's interests in intelligence, prior to the battle?*

Just prior to the Midway operation, Vice-Admiral Chuichi Nagumo, the Commander-in-Chief of the First Mobile Fleet, assessed the enemy (i.e., the US) as follows: "The US Navy is demoralized; therefore, the US carriers won't appear for the time being. It will be only after the domination of the Midway Islands by our Imperial Navy that the US carriers will appear in this area." This was an arbitrary judgment based on biased preconceptions without concrete information about the movements of the US aircraft carrier task forces. Commanders should avoid such groundless presumptions when there is not enough information to assess the situation at hand before ordering intelligence activities; Vice-Admiral Nagumo, however, somehow fell into this trap.

In contrast, Admiral Isoroku Yamamoto, the Commander-in-Chief of the Grand Fleet, was on high alert and assessed the situation

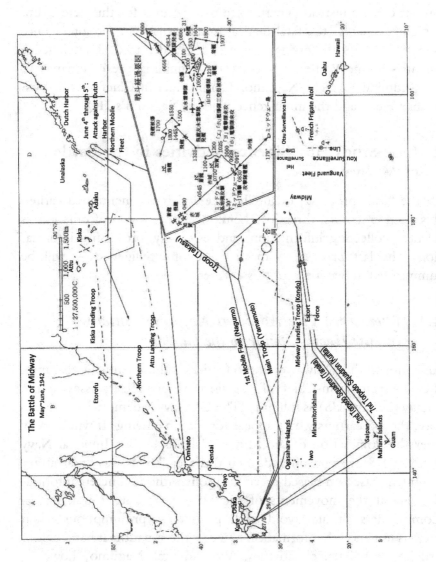

Figure 33:   The Battle of Midway

thus: "The US Navy's fighting spirit is high. Even though they lost eight main battleships in the Pearl Harbor surprise attack during the early stages of this war, the US aircraft carrier mobile units have repeatedly engaged in aggressive local attacks. We must capture and destroy them as soon as possible." Therefore, his plan was to use the Midway operation to lure the US aircraft carriers out and annihilate them all at once.

Thus, Admiral Yamamoto and Vice-Admiral Nagumo differed greatly not just in their assessment of the situation, but also in their understanding of the operation's objectives. With historical hindsight, we can say that this difference in fundamental views caused the failure of the Midway operation, and it was also why Vice-Admiral Nagumo misjudged the need for intelligence.

Undoubtedly, the failure of communication between the Supreme Commander (Admiral Yamamoto) and the commander of the task force (Vice-Admiral Nagumo) regarding the operation's objectives was the ultimate cause of the defeat in the Battle of Midway. This difference in assessment of the opponent adversely influenced the first process of intelligence activities ("deciding what information is needed") for Nagumo's First Mobile Fleet. Vice-Admiral Nagumo estimated that there was little possibility that the US aircraft carrier mobile fleets were operating in the area; his interest in intelligence activities therefore lay in the success of the Midway operation, not in the whereabouts of the US carrier task forces. Thus, the initial reconnoitering plan of Nagumo's fleet was just a precautionary measure, not a serious reconnaissance operation.

4.2. Was Nagumo's fleet's reconnoitering operation against the US aircraft carrier mobile fleets adequate?

On June 5, 1942, the Nagumo Fleet sent a few planes on a reconnaissance mission for the Midway operation. This was a mere precautionary measure, not a proper, thorough recon mission for target acquisition, as shown in Figure 34. How could the staff of the First Mobile Fleet, supposed to be the very best of the naval elites, conduct such a haphazard recon mission?

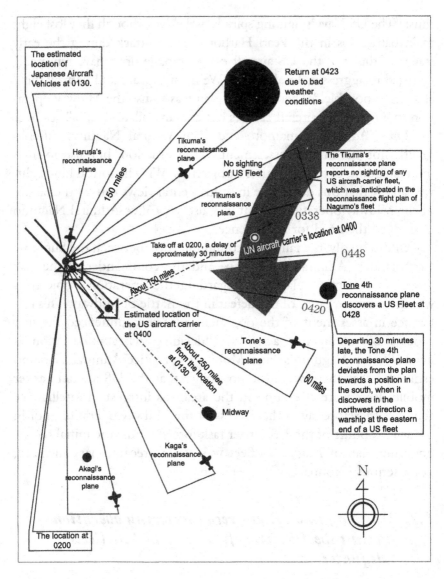

Figure 34: Outline of the Surveillance Activities Carried Out by Nagumo's Fleet on June 5, 1942

Box 1 provides a play-by-play summary of Vice-Admiral Nagumo's tactical commands on June 5th. At 1:30 a.m. that day, just before dawn, Vice-Admiral Nagumo ordered the attack unit consisting of 103 planes to take off, and at the same time, seven recon seaplanes to take off as well to reconnoiter the areas surrounding the fleet. What is incomprehensible is that only seven recon planes were sent, though the fleet possessed many recon seaplanes. Evidently, Nagumo's HQ did not think to make use of the golden rule in naval combat, "early detection of the enemy's aircraft carrier," which they only discovered later from experience in battle.

What is even more incomprehensible is the decision Vice-Admiral Nagumo made when recon seaplane No. 4 onboard the heavy cruiser "Tone" could not depart on time because of catapult failure. As mentioned previously, timeliness of reporting is of utmost importance in intelligence activities. For some reason, however, instead of quickly using a reserve recon plane, Nagumo ordered repairs to be made to No. 4. As a result, recon plane No. 4 took off half an hour later at 2:00 a.m. It did not find the US fleet on the outward journey, but did manage to find it on the return journey. However, there was a mix-up with the flight plan, and No. 4 reported its current location wrongly; the US fleet was reported to be further away from the Nagumo fleet than was actually the case (about 90 nautical miles).

4.3. *Did Nagumo's HQ properly process information?*

At 4:00 a.m., Nagumo's HQ received a telegram from the commander of the first strike squadron of the Midway Atoll, reporting the necessity for the second attack on the Midway islands. There was still no sighting of the enemy fleet by 4:15 a.m., when the six recon planes (except No. 4) were expected to have reached the end of the planned search zones. Therefore, Nagumo, judging that there was no US fleet in the vicinity of the search zones, decided to go ahead with the second strike on Midway Atoll.

The US forces based in Midway Atoll began a series of attacks on the Nagumo Fleet at 4:05 a.m., five minutes after the Nagumo HQ

Box 1:   Vice-Admiral Nagumo's Tactical Commands (June 5, 1942, JST 0130~)

Sunrise: 0152, Sunset: 1548

Japanese forces	*American forces

0130:   Air Defense Interceptors, Air Attack Squadrons, Reconnaissance Planes take off.
*US 17th Task Force's reconnaissance planes take off.

0200:   The 4th reconnaissance plane departs 30 minutes late.

0220:   Vice-Admiral Nagumo issues the preparatory command "to carry out the assault against Midway Base, if no change occurs in the combat situation."

*US reconnaissance plane discovers IJN's aircraft carrier.

0232:   **Nagumo's Fleet confronts a US reconnaissance plane.**

0253:   *Midway's radar detects IJN's Air Attack Squadron.
Order is immediately issued for all Midway planes to attack IJN's aircraft carrier.

0255:   The 4th reconnaissance plane reports "fifteen US air-planes flying towards us."
Nagumo judges at once that these planes are from Midway.

0334:   The First Attack Squadron commences attacks against the US Midway Base.

0400:   The commander of the First Attack Squadron radios the message, **"We should carry out the second strike against Midway."**

*TF16 issues the command to consecutively dispatch attack planes.

0405–0540:   Due to consecutive raids and aerial defense operations of Midway's planes, a major part of the fighter airplanes of the Second Attack Squadron is used. Most of the US planes are shot down, while the Japanese forces suffer no casualties.

Box 1: (*Continued*)

0415:	Friendly reconnaissance plane reports nothing regarding US Fleet activities.
	Vice-Admiral Nagumo decides to attack the Midway Base, ordering the conversion of the weaponry already equipped in the Second Attack Squadron's planes.
0428:	The 4th reconnaissance plane reports the discovery of what appear to be ten US warships at ten degrees, 240 miles from Midway, at a latitude of 150 degrees.
0445:	The 4th reconnaissance plane reports the weather conditions around the US Fleet.
	Nagumo judges the US Fleet to include an aircraft carrier, and the range to be about 240 miles between the US fleet and his. Nagumo goes on to order the re-equipment of weapons.
0450:	Fighters of the First Attack Squadron return from the Midway, one after another.
0509:	The 4th reconnaissance plane reports, "The US Fleet includes 5 cruisers and 5 destroyers."
0520:	The 4th reconnaissance plane reports the likelihood that "the US Fleet includes an aircraft carrier." The Deputy Commander Admiral Yamaguchi states, "All planes should take off immediately."
	Vice-Admiral Nagumo decides to accommodate the First Attack Squadron from the Midway for re-equipping and refueling prior to attacking the enemy carrier. At the same time, he also decides to head north.
0530:	2nd type reconnaissance plane is dispatched to search for the US aircraft carrier.
0540–0618:	US air assault ends and almost all friendly planes land safely on the Japanese aircraft carrier.
0618:	US carries out aerial attacks from their aircraft carrier, but almost all of them are shot down by Japanese fighters.
0700:	2nd type reconnaissance plane fails to report to Nagumo that there is no sighting of the US Fleet in the area reported by the 4th reconnaissance plane.

Box 1:   (*Continued*)

0723:	At the moment of intercepting US Torpedo planes, other US bombers carry out aerial bombardments against Akagi, Kaga, and Soryu, causing casualties.
0730:	US air assault ends.
0746:	Vice-Admiral Nagumo moves from the Akagi to the Nagara.
0748:	The Hiryu's First Attack Squadron (18 bombers and 6 fighters) take off to carry out raids against the US Air Mobile Fleet.
0900:	The raid of Hiryu's First Attack Squadron against the US aircraft carrier succeeds.
1031:	The Hiryu's Second Attack Squadron (10 torpedo planes and 6 fighters) take off. Subsequently, the First Squadron returns.
1145:	The Hiryu's Second Squadron shoots 2 torpedoes that directly hit the US aircraft carrier.
1245:	The Hiryu's Second Squadron returns to the aircraft carrier.
1330:	Admiral Yamaguchi reports to Nagumo that the Third Attack Squadron will take off at 1500.

received the telegram described above. Although the US attacks on the Nagumo Fleet lasted for about an hour and a half until 5:40 a.m., the Nagumo Fleet deployed most of the fighter airplanes in its second strike squadron and successfully shot down the majority of the enemy planes. There was a significant gap in aerial combat ability between the IJN and the US Navy back then.

What is problematic here, however, is that Vice-Admiral Nagumo, of his own volition, without obtaining permission from the Commander-in-Chief of the Grand Fleet, ordered a change of equipment for the second strike squadron from fleet attack equipment (torpedoes and anti-ship missiles) to land-attack missiles. This was in violation of the order from the Grand Fleet which banned any change of equipment for the second attack units.

At 4:28 a.m., 13 minutes after ordering re-equipment, Vice-Admiral Nagumo received a telegram from recon plane No. 4 stating that it had discovered 10 suspected enemy ships in position bearing 10 degrees, 240 miles away from Midway, at a latitude of 150 degrees. Nagumo, having already assumed that the US fleets were not operating in the vicinity, doubted the credibility of this report and decided to wait for a new report instead. Although this report was wrong in its location, no one in the HQ suspected this, which turned out to be a flagrant blunder.

What the intelligence staff at HQ should have done was immediately assess the relevance of this information, and issue a new order for locating the current position of the US fleet. Then, they should have immediately assessed the credibility and accuracy of the information, thereby turning it into intelligence, and thereafter reported it to the Commander-in-Chief without further delay.

To reiterate: when the intelligence staff first received the telegram from recon plane No. 4, they should have first of all assessed the relevance of this information. As mentioned earlier, Nagumo's HQ did not anticipate the appearance of the US fleet in the vicinity, in its original assessment of the situation prior to the battle. Therefore, it must have recognized the significance of this telegram which overturned all its previous assumptions. Upon receiving the report, it should have re-focused its intelligence assets and activities on ascertaining the truth about the enemy fleet. That is to say, Nagumo's HQ should have immediately sent a reserve recon plane to the area where No. 4 reportedly sighted the US fleet, and at the same time, re-equipped its own fleet with torpedoes and anti-ship missiles. However, Nagumo only sent the reserve plane 62 minutes later, and ordered re-equipment 17 minutes later.

Next, Nagumo's HQ should have examined the credibility of the telegram. The ambiguity of the report ("what appears to be the enemy"), in truth, should have cast suspicion over the recon pilot's intelligence ability. There is no trace, however, of the agent's ability being called into question. As for the critical information, i.e., the type of ships, the pilot reported that "the enemy is accompanied by what appears to be a carrier," only after being urged by the HQ.

This greatly invites distrust of the pilot's ability as an intelligence agent. If the HQ staff had only checked the reported position against the planned route, it would have taken a mere second for them to have some doubts about the pilot's locating ability. Given that the reported position was not on the planned route, the intelligence staff should have requested the pilot to reconfirm the report, and at the same time, they should have sent another recon plane to double-check the accuracy of the information.

Thus, the accuracy of the reported position ("in position bearing 10 degrees, 240 miles away from Midway, at a latitude of 150 degrees") should have been immediately called into question, as it was not on the planned route in the flight plan for the recon mission. This failure to notice the pilot's mistake regarding the reported position resulted in Vice-Admiral Nagumo's fatal errors in strategic management: sending the fleet northward into the reach of the US aircraft carriers' attack, and missing the chance to win the battle whilst postponing attacks on the enemy fleet.

The critical error in the processing of information in this case was simply that the intelligence staff failed to follow the basic procedure in analyzing the raw information and processing it into intelligence, before communicating it to the commander. Only after receiving another report from recon plane No. 4 regarding the weather conditions in the area at 4:45 a.m., 17 minutes after the first telegram, did Vice-Admiral Nagumo believe the first report. Nagumo then finally ordered No. 4 to confirm the type of ships and to continue surveillance. He also decided to attack the US fleet, and ordered re-equipment for fleet attack.

At 5:09 a.m., 41 minutes after the first telegram, recon plane No. 4 reported that the enemy fleet consisted of five cruisers and five destroyers. Then, 11 minutes later at 5:20 a.m., the pilot reported again that the enemy fleet was accompanied by what appeared to be an aircraft carrier. At this stage, Rear-Admiral Tamon Yamaguchi, the second-in-command of the fleet, was alerted to the gravity of the situation and offered his opinion that the IJN needed to attack the US aircraft carrier immediately. However, Vice-Admiral Nagumo decided to wait for the return of the first strike squadron, before mounting a well-prepared attack on the enemy fleet and annihilating it. Not questioning the accuracy of the fleet location as reported by recon plane No. 4, he presumed that the US fleet was still far away and that he had enough time to prepare for an attack.

At 5:30 a.m., Nagumo's fleet sent a type 2 carrier-based reconnaissance plane onboard the Soryu, an aircraft carrier, for further reconnaissance. This was only after a significant time period of 62 minutes had lapsed since the first telegram from recon plane No. 4. Not surprisingly, the type 2 recon plane failed to locate the enemy fleet, as the reported position was wrong in the first place. To make matters worse, the telegram from this plane stating that it could not find the enemy fleet did not reach the HQ, due to a technical problem with radio communication.

Having already ordered re-equipment for fleet attack, Vice-Admiral Nagumo ordered his fleet to proceed north in order to shorten the distance between themselves and the enemy fleet. The plan was to capture and destroy the enemy fleet at one fell stroke. However, he did not examine the accuracy of the reported position, and instead used that raw collected information for tactical decision-making.

Of course, it has to be taken into account that all of this was done in the midst of a chaotic situation where the IJN had to engage in air combat against the US aircrafts from Midway Atoll, and re-equip aircrafts on its own carriers. This, nonetheless, was not out of the norm in a battlefield; rather, it was the usual state of affairs in battle. Under however much psychological pressure, a military commander is required to assume ultimate responsibility for the consequences of every single decision he or she makes. In hindsight, it has to be said that Vice-Admiral Nagumo exposed his fleet to unnecessary risk and danger by willingly entering into the reach of attack of the US aircraft carrier mobile unit.

5. Summary

At the beginning of this chapter, I pointed out that the purpose of military intelligence activities is to minimize the unknown factors regarding the enemy, to aid in commanders' situation assessment and decision-making. Here, I would like to review each procedure we have examined in the previous sections, through the process of "Making use of intelligence." In the Battle of Midway, was the information required by Vice-Admiral Nagumo for his tactical decision-making appropriate and provided in a timely manner?

We reviewed the manner in which Nagumo's HQ processed information during the Battle of Midway, by tracking the Vice-Admiral's orders. From the viewpoint of "use of intelligence," the biggest failure in the Battle of Midway was that the intelligence staff reported the information provided by recon plane No. 4 directly to the commander, without processing the information into intelligence. This mistake occurred because Vice-Admiral Nagumo did not require any information related to the possibility of the US carrier fleet's presence in the area. Since his main interest in intelligence activities was how to secure victory in attacking Midway Atoll, officers at the HQ had little interest in reconnoitering for the potential presence of a US carrier fleet. Therefore, both the recon work (collecting information) and the reporting (processing of information) lacked alacrity.

It can thus be concluded that what dictates the entire intelligence activities in strategy and battle is the timely, correct and clear setting down of intelligence requirements by the commander. In the case of the Battle of Midway, Vice-Admiral Nagumo's inadequate intelligence requirements led to all the subsequent failures in the intelligence activities. The cause of this inadequacy was his lack of understanding of the operation's objectives. Here, the responsibility for Nagumo's lack of understanding must lie with the supreme commander, Admiral Yamamoto, the Commander-in-Chief of the Grand Fleet, who did not make enough of an effort to ensure that Nagumo fully understood the operation's objectives.

It is clear that the difference in views between the Supreme Commander and the front-line commander regarding the operation's objectives played a critical role from the beginning; yet, it was imperative that the intelligence staff surrounding the commander acted professionally too, perhaps by suggesting a change in the commander's initial intelligence requirements. Failing that, the intelligence staff should still have been committed to detecting any potential enemy action in the final process of "making use of intelligence." They should have at least analyzed what enemy action would gravely impact the operation, e.g., potential surprise attacks by the enemy. Whether information is successfully collected or not, this responsibility to expect the unexpected and warn the commander against it is the most important duty of intelligence staff.

Postscript

Ever since I was stationed in New York as Vice President, Business Development, Nichimen America Inc., I have duly recognized the importance of business intelligence. Therefore, upon returning to Tokyo from New York, I established the Business Intelligence Society of Japan in February 1992. Since then, I have made my very best effort to study and introduce business and competitive intelligence in Japan in my role as President of the above society.

For this purpose, I have translated and published the following books in Japanese: Herbert E. Meyer's *Real-World Intelligence* from Diamond Publishing Company; Benjamin and Tamal Gilad's *The Business Intelligence System* from Eruko; and William V. Rapp's *Information Technology Strategy* from Nikkei BP. I have also contributed my own articles and writing in books such as *The Intelligent Corporation* from Taylor Graham, London, UK; and *Global Perspectives on Competitive Intelligence* from the Society of Competitive Intelligence Professionals, Alexandria, Virginia, USA.

However, much to my regret, there has not been much interest in business and competitive intelligence in Japan. In comparison with Europe and the USA, the study of business intelligence has not advanced far in Japan. The influential book, *The Business Intelligence*, published in France and written by Bernard Liautaud and Mark Hammond, was translated into Japanese and published in Japan by Shoeisha. However, even this could not attract the interest of the Japanese people. On the contrary, recently, many books on diplomacy, international politics and military intelligence have been published in Japan. The word "Intelligence" is often cited in these books, but it has no relation to business intelligence.

Taking into consideration the recent world financial crisis, business intelligence — which refers to value-added and highly advanced economic, business and financial intelligence — should become an imperative tool in the field of global business, under which the severe global competition has been much intensified.

It is therefore very good and opportune timing that the Business Intelligence Society of Japan (BISJ) has published this unique book, *An Introduction to Knowledge Information Strategy: From Business Intelligence to Knowledge Sciences*, with the esteemed cooperation of the researchers, academia and distinguished business experts who make up the members of BISJ, in commemoration of its 100th meeting on the 18th anniversary since it was founded in 1992. We, the writers, will be very happy if this book can contribute to the dissemination of the concept and practice of business intelligence, and furthermore, to strengthening the global competitiveness of the Japanese corporations in the world market.

Last but not least, we extend our heartfelt gratitude for the recommendation of this book to Mr. Kakutaro Kitashiro, senior adviser of Japan IBM; and also to Mr. Hideo Yokoyama, former President of Eruko, for his esteemed advice and cooperation in editing this book. Further thanks go to Mr. Eiji Minemura, General Manager of Division 3, and to Mr. Shinichiro Okawa of Zeimu Keiri Kyokai.

November 2012
Juro Nakagawa, co-editor and author
President, Business Intelligence Society of Japan

Index